The road to

Teen Vision

The road to

Teen Vision

How to find
your passion
and realize
your dreams

kristi stoll & gidget clayton

BEYOND
WORDS
Publishing
I N C

Published by
Beyond Words Publishing, Inc.
20827 NW Cornell Road, Suite 500
Hillsboro, Oregon 97124
503-531-8700

Editors: Barbara Leese, Kristin Hilton, Summer Steele
Proofreader: Jade Chan
Interior Design: Jerry Soga
Layout: William H. Brunson Typography Services

ISBN: 1-58270-117-2

Printed in the United States of America
Distributed to the book trade by Publishers Group West

Library of Congress Cataloging-in-Publication Data

Stoll, Kristi.
    Teen vision / by Kristi Stoll and Gidget Clayton.
        p. cm.
    1. Teenagers—Conduct of life.   I. Clayton, Gidget.   II. Title.

    BJ1661.S86   2005
    170'.835—dc22

                                        2004015466

The corporate mission of Beyond Words Publishing, Inc:
    Inspire to Integrity

table of contents

We live in a world influenced daily by kids with vision, kids who are accomplishing their goals and living out their amazing dreams. Inspired by the courageous and creative spirits of kids who choose to follow their vision and fulfill their dreams, we were motivated to honor our own dream of sharing their stories with others. Gidget sold everything and bought an RV, and the two of us traveled for about ten months all across the country, interviewing amazing kids along the way. This book is both a gift to you, the reader—a guide to help you realize that anything is possible—and a gift to us—proof that dreams really do come true.

Do You Have TeenViʌion?

We guess you need to know what TeenVision is to know if you have it or not, right?

To begin with, TeenVision has five basic ingredients. TeenVision starts with having a *dream* or vision of what you would like to accomplish. Second, it's all about sharing your *inner gifts*—the special talents you possess and the unique way you communicate them. Next is finding your *passion*—the feeling that motivates you. Fourth, it's believing in the *magic* of a dream—or that anything is possible. And last but not least, a very important part of TeenVision is having *guts*—the willingness to put yourself and your idea out there. And there you have it: that's TeenVision!

So who has TeenVision? *Everyone.* Yes, everyone—including YOU! TeenVision isn't just for teens; it's for anyone whose heart is filled with the hope and spark of dreaming—the sort of dreaming that will one day lead you to accomplish your ultimate goal, whatever that may be. This book has been created to help you find your own vision, discover your dreams, uncover your inner gifts, and to help you believe in them as well. No matter what stage you're at, this book can guide you on your dream path. Remember, the world needs you, your talents, and your ideas, so never give up. We believe in you and we want you to succeed!

To keep you inspired, each chapter includes a motivational interview with someone like you who followed his or her own vision. These are stories about young people from all across the country who were interviewed in person, especially for you, to show you the magic that can happen when you follow your dreams. These sections, titled "LET'S DO IT!" will show you how these young people's visions came to life, the steps they took to make their dreams a reality, and advice they have for you to help you follow your own dream.

As you read this book, find yourself in its pages. See yourself in the faces of the kids out there who are already living their vision. Get inspired and get excited, because you truly are a gift and the world can't wait to see what you have to share!

At the end of the book you will find a chapter dedicated solely to you! This is where you have the chance to write your own story or write about your own visions and dreams. Each chapter of the book will guide you on how to fill out the different sections in your own chapter, but if you feel inspired, you don't have to wait; go ahead and start writing!

By the way, there is no right or wrong way to read this book. If you want to read it through from beginning to end, great. But feel free to skip to the chapters and stories that sound most appealing to you. Every section is designed to get you thinking about the fabulous gifts and visions you have to share.

Are you ready? Come on, let's go!

Meet Kri∧ti and Gidget

Kri∧ti: I would describe myself as a dreamer, an idealist, a seeker of truth, and someone who looks at life in terms of the big picture. My favorite things in life are laughing, having fun, connecting with and helping people, interacting with nature and animals, and learning about and exploring new things.

People tell me that they are inspired by my faith in the universe. When I think back, I guess some of the decisions I have made, like quitting a steady job and career to move across the country to California with only $60 in my pocket and the total faith that everything would work out, may not be choices that others would make. But regardless, my faith and positive outlook always get me where I want to be.

Gidget: I am an artist, photographer, crafter, and undeclared risk taker; prior to starting this project, however, I would not have described myself like that at all. I was afraid of everything and worried about what I should and shouldn't be doing and how I should do it. But through the process of interviewing and writing about all the amazing kids in this book, I renewed my belief systems and now find myself not caring so much about what other people think. I have changed so much. I am now a person who believes that I can do anything. I believe in my dreams and my ability to succeed in life. I still say that I am not a risk taker, but in reality I take risks every day. It's just that it isn't until I've taken and completed them that I acknowledge that they were risks.

What wa∧ your in∧piration for writing The Road to TeenVi∧ion?

Gidget: One day I stayed home sick from work and watched *Oprah*. She had several kids on the show who were very inspiring. There was an eight-year-old who collected suitcases for foster kids, a ten-year-old genius who advocated world peace, and a nine-year-old who formed a peer group to help spread the word of nonviolence. I began to wonder what the process for success was for these kids. I really wanted to know so that I could take the information and apply it to my own life. It really wasn't just about the success but about their courage to start and complete their goals without knowing exactly how to do it. I had been looking for direction ever since I had lost myself to a corporate job and the day-to-day grind of adult life. I needed a guide to follow in order to accomplish the dreams that I had tucked away in a far, far place. These kids inspired me to find my passions and follow my dreams; I thought that they would be great examples for others. That's when I decided that I needed to share what I had learned from them.

Kristi: I wanted to create an encouraging and motivating book for young people that not only demonstrates the "how" of connecting with their dreams, talents, and inner gifts, but also provides the required resources for finding the courage, guidance, and confidence necessary to achieve those dreams.

My inspiration came one night as I was sitting up with a friend to await some news from her family. Around 3:00 AM, we were watching TV to pass the time, and a talk show came on about teens. As I watched the show, it dawned on me how unsupported some kids are when it comes to discovering their true talents and inner gifts. It saddens me to think that sometimes a dream can get locked inside a person and perhaps never surface, or that some kids know they have a dream but don't have any encouragement to explore it. Even still, there are other kids out there who don't know that having a dream is even a possibility.

While watching the broken spirits of some of these kids, something inside me transformed. It was at that moment that I knew I needed to work with kids at all stages of their lives and support and encourage them to hold on to their magic and brilliance—their inner light. My hope is that readers can use this book as a launching pad to discovering more about themselves. I also hope it will be a source of support and inspiration for making choices that fill their hearts with joy, passion, and fulfillment.

How did you get started?

Kristi: It all began when I moved back to California, where Gidget lived. Gidget and I were friends from work and had kept in touch over the years. Both of us were going through a transitional time in our lives and looking for new opportunities.

Gidget: One day I called Kristi and told her that I wanted to sell everything, buy an RV, and travel across the country to interview kids about their dreams.

Kristi: Without having to think about it, I knew that this idea was meant to be, so I told Gidget that I was in! The next thing we knew, we had sold everything and were headed out in our RV, starting a new adventure.

What was involved in writing The Road to TeenVision?

Kristi: We traveled in the RV from California, through Arizona, and into Colorado, where we stayed with family to save some money while we were getting started. We are so grateful for the help and support from our families and friends. I'm not sure we would have ever accomplished everything we did without them.

Gidget: The first thing we did was create a Web site [http://www.PlanetGiggle.com] where people could read about us and follow along on our trek across the country. We also started compiling information on a variety of amazing kids from around the country. We didn't have all the money we needed, so we stayed in Colorado and worked some odd jobs to fund our trip.

Kristi: While staying in Colorado, we set up our first interview in Denver. We decided to videotape all the interviews so that we could be sure to capture the entire experience. We were a little nervous since we had never interviewed anyone before, but it couldn't have turned out better if I had scripted the answers myself. The feeling we had about how well the interview went fueled us to keep going. It was great! After that first interview, we knew this could turn out to be something really amazing and inspirational.

Gidget: Once we got enough money together and had a good idea of which kids we wanted to interview, we headed back out on the road. As we traveled, we contacted kids along the way to see who was interested in participating in the book.

Kristi: We traveled in our RV from Colorado to Florida, up through the northeast and back to California—a total of twenty-three states. Once home, the funds from a temporary consulting job enabled us to travel via plane to our last two interviews in Oregon and Chicago.

Gidget: After we were finished with all the interviews, we had the videotapes transcribed and began looking for a publisher.

How did you find all the kids you interviewed?

Gidget: Each interviewee in the book was someone we found on the Internet, read about in a newspaper, saw on TV, or came as a word-of-mouth recommendation.

How did you find a publisher?

Kristi: We began by researching other books intended for our target market and then found out who published them. We got lucky when we heard about a large book expo— where anyone who has anything to do with publishing gathers—in L.A. Not only were we able to see the entire publishing industry up close and personal, but we also came away with several prospective publishers whose mission statements matched our message.

Gidget: After we had our list of publishers, we created a book proposal and sent it out. Within about five months we found a publisher and started writing the text that you are reading today.

How long has it taken you to interview the kids and write the book?

Kristi: The entire process has taken three years. It's been an amazing journey. We've learned so much along the way. It's true that doors open up where you never knew they existed and obstacles do arise that must be overcome. But if you keep your eye on the big picture and stay focused on your dream, really anything *is* possible. Gidget and I are more than excited and proud to be presenting this book to you today. We hope everyone enjoys the interviews as much as we do.

What changes have you seen within yourself throughout this project?

Gidget: During this project my drive and passion have changed focus. The project began as a journey of self-exploration but evolved into one that was focused on the amazing kids we found. The funny thing is, these kids are just like any other kids. The difference seems to be in their personal belief systems. How they feel about themselves is what seems to make all the difference. I see what these kids did and now know that because I did not believe enough in myself or my abilities to get past any obstacles, I didn't initially succeed in living my dream. I would come up against an obstacle and stop. I would say to myself, "Who am I to overcome this? Who am I to change how this has been done in the past?" My self-defeating thoughts took over and created a belief system that did not support me and who I truly was.

After interviewing each kid, I would think, "Wow, what an amazing perspective for someone who is so young." Now I realize that their way of thinking is natural and that mine was based on what happens when you go outside of yourself for your belief systems and worry about what other people think of you.

Kristi: I've seen a lot of changes within myself throughout the life of this project. Most have to do with my ability to communicate and connect with others, my confidence in myself and my work, and my exponential spiritual growth.

What has been the most and least fun you have had throughout this experience?

Gidget: Looking back on all that has happened from the start until now, I would say that the little moments that Kristi and I shared laughing and having fun are my most cherished times. One time, while taking a walk at an RV campsite, Kristi wanted to explore an area that had been fenced off. I told her that the fence was an electric fence. I had told her this several other times throughout the trip and none of them were electrical fences. She held the top wire down so that she could jump over it and got a pretty good jolt. We both started laughing uncontrollably. It was nice to be able to have fun while we traveled and worked.

I would say the least amount of fun that I had was setting up and tearing down the RV systems, like the holding tank. If you think about it, what goes in must come out. Yuck!

Kristi: The most fun was traveling and seeing new things and listening to the wisdom that the kids we interviewed had to share. The least fun has been the obstacles, which are too numerous to mention, that we have had to overcome to share this book with you.

What have you learned from the kids you interviewed?

Gidget: I have learned that instead of letting it stop you, fear can be used to help you. Fear can create and guide the path in a negative way or fear can help you find a different path that will lead you to your dreams. A person's beliefs are bigger than any obstacles he or she might face. I also learned that no matter what anyone else thinks of my ideas or me, I alone have the ability to change the world and myself. The key to my own success lies in my beliefs about myself and the world around me.

Kristi: I learned that the power of having support in your life can mean the difference between succeeding at a dream and not succeeding, as well as the difference between feeling the freedom and courage to do anything you want, and not feeling freedom and courage at all. I learned how amazingly wise young people are and how awesome it can be to connect with them and hear their stories. I loved watching the kids light up when they spoke about their creations. I think it is so important for people to be able to have the opportunity to do something they love.

What is your dream?

Gidget: I have so many dreams. Every day it seems like I add a new one. Writing and publishing *The Road to TeenVision* was one of my dreams, and guess what—I did it! Also, writing pictures books for little kids and being a professional photographer have both been dreams of mine ever since I was very young. I have so many dreams!

Kristi: My dream is that every person can grow up knowing what talents, gifts, creativity, and magic he or she possesses. Imagine how different this world would be if that were so! My mission in this world is to be a voice of change that inspires others to want to look within themselves to discover the beauty, the genius, and the gifts they possess. I also have many personal dreams, which include traveling the world, exploring and learning everything there is to explore and learn, writing songs, playing the guitar ... and so much more!

This book is the culmination of an eight-year journey that took me from working in the corporate world to quitting my job to pursue my dreams, to learning about myself and my inner gifts and finally discovering the message I needed to share with others. When I first quit my job, it was to pursue a dream very similar to writing this book, but for various reasons I was forced to put that dream on the back burner. Now, eight years later, it has come full circle, which I believe is a testament to everything this book is about.

I get excited when I see people become aware of the possibilities that exist within themselves to do something that they love to do. In the exact moment that they connect with their inner gifts and possibilities, it is as if a light turns on. That light is what connects us to one another. It is both magical and an honor to have the opportunity to inspire others to find and share the messages in their heart, which is their light. This book is my opportunity to share my light with you, and my hope is that you will feel as inspired when you read it as we did when we wrote it.

What is your message to others?

Gidget: My message to anyone, whether adult or kid, is "get to know yourself." Find out what your belief systems really are. Question everything and take responsibility for your actions. And last but not least, never, never stop dreaming!

Kristi: Know that you possess a magical gift that no one else holds and that that gift is intended to be utilized and shared. Trust your inner guidance to lead you to where you need to be. Know that you are not alone. Travel and explore new things any chance you get—it opens up your world. Dream big and know that you absolutely can achieve anything. People have told me that I can't be an instrument of change because the world doesn't want to change, but I already know in my heart that I can bring change, and that makes all the difference. Be willing to be yourself, listen to and share the message in your heart, and then watch how YOU change the world.

section 1

Dreams

Dreams

A dream is an idea or vision you have about what you would like to be or do in the future. Usually a dream is something that you feel very passionate about achieving. A dream could be creating a project that helps people or animals, starting your own company, inventing something, or becoming a recording artist, an actor, or a professional sports player. These are just a few ideas of what a dream can be. There are no limits to *your* dream.

Did you know that the visions or dreams you have might be an idea that no one else has had yet? Think about it: new things are created only when someone first dreams up the idea, right? So when you get those ideas that you think someone else has already thought of, think again. Your vision could actually be a new discovery or something extraordinary that is meant to be shared with the rest of us.

In this section, we'll help you define your dream and discover how you can believe in your power to achieve it. These are the essential first steps toward making your dream come true.

CHAPTER 1

Find Your Dreams

Finding your dream takes imagination and inspiration. Do you know what inspiration feels like? Give this a try. Close your eyes and imagine seeing yourself doing something you totally love doing. It can be anything—hanging out with friends, playing your favorite sport, or listening to music. Notice how you feel when you are envisioning this. Are you happy, excited, proud, energized, or all these feelings at once? It feels great, doesn't it?

This is what inspiration feels like. Remember this feeling—the amazing feeling you get when you connect with inspiration—because you will use it as your guide to find your dreams.

To find your dreams, think about anything you have wanted to do or goals you have wanted to accomplish. Focus on what you love to do, what you're good at, what you feel would make a difference in the world, or even what you think would be awesome to experience. Your dreams can be any-thing; just let the ideas flow. For example, have you ever dreamed of being a singer or an artist? How about working with animals, elderly people, or kids? Do you want to invent something, start a business, or take an existing idea and make it better? What about cleaning up the environment or collecting toys or food for people who are in need? How about exploring different cultures, learning different lan-guages, or studying different ancient histories? These are all visions; the ones we've listed here are general ideas, but yours will be unique to you, so don't limit your ideas to our suggestions.

✍ Start a list of your ideas because we will work with them throughout the book. In fact, you can skip to the "My TeenVision" chapter and write down your dreams. You might have one dream or you might have many. There is no wrong way to dream and there are no stupid dreams, so let the ideas come and write them all down. If you don't want to write in this book, make photocopies of the pages in your chapter, staple them together, and use them as a private journal.

By now, you should have one or more dreams written down. Look over your list. Remember that feeling of inspiration we discussed earlier? You are going to use it now. Go down your list and focus on each dream for a minute. As you are focusing, imagine yourself in that dream. Really see yourself in each dream. Are you getting that happy, excited feeling? (If not, that's OK.) ✍ Make a note, perhaps by placing a star, next to the dreams that give you an inspired feeling. These are the ones you will concentrate on for now.

You want to focus on the dreams that give you a feeling of inspiration because that feeling is your guide. Your inspiration keeps you connected to the passion, excitement, and motivation you need to keep following your dream. It's a compass that will point you in the right direction. If you don't feel inspired by a particular dream, it's probably not worth pursuing—at least for now. If you are ever in doubt about whether you are doing the right thing or making the right decision, always look for this feeling. It will steer you in the right direction. If you're not sure that you are feeling inspiration right now, don't worry. By the end of the book you will have a good understanding of how to tap into your inspiration and use it as your guide.

You should now have a list of dreams and a star next to the ones that you feel excited about. If not, keep reading and don't get discouraged. This is a great starting place and there is much more to come that will help you. Maybe our interview with Keisha McDaniel, founder of the Pretty

Tomboy clothing line, will inspire you to explore all the possibilities available to you.

LET'S DO IT!

Keisha McDaniel

Age 15
Las Vegas, Nevada

clothing Designer
and founder of
pretty Tomboy
clothing

**"Be yourself or please
everyone else!"**

We met Keisha at her home in Las Vegas, Nevada. Her room
reflected the life of a typical teenager: sports trophies lined
up in one corner, a closet full of sneakers, and the ener-
getic beat of hip-hop playing in the background. Keisha is
a very confident teenager. She expresses her dreams with
so much enthusiasm that it made us want to be a part of
that energy.

Meet Keisha

Keisha was in beauty pageants when she was three years
old. As she got older, she decided that pageants weren't her
thing and moved on to sports and bigger, baggier clothes. At
that time, girls' clothes didn't stretch for sports, so all that
was available to her, in a fit and style she liked, were boys'
clothes. But when she wore them, people made fun of her
and called her names. Her mom, Joyce, wanted Keisha to
know that she could do something other than wear boys'
clothes or tight-fitting girls' clothes, so Joyce had Keisha
create a clothing design. Keisha's first designs were made

into comfortable clothes in colors like yellow and pink. This change helped Keisha's self-esteem a lot.

K&G: How did you start your own clothing line?

I was nine when the idea of creating my own clothing came up. It started because at that stage of my life, I wasn't happy in dresses. I liked baggy clothes, so that meant wearing boys' clothes but people made fun of me for wearing them. I remember this exactly. I asked my mom, "Why does everybody bother me so much? Why does everybody call me names?" My mom said, "Go design a t-shirt and put what you want on it." I went to my room and I tried to draw a dog. It didn't work out, but then I tried drawing a paw print. That was my first design. Later, I developed a whole line of clothing. I named it Pretty Tomboy Clothing. It's for all women. You don't have to be a tomboy or even a pretty tomboy to wear it.

K&G: Why did you name your clothing line Pretty Tomboy Clothing?

The clothes started out with the name KeeDog Clothing. KeeDog is my nickname. Later we changed it to Pretty Tomboy— "tomboy" for girls who get called "tomboy" because of the clothes they wear, and "pretty" because I'm pretty and we wanted to show girls that you can be a tomboy and still be pretty, too. [So, that's why] we sold t-shirts that had "Pretty Tomboy" on them. My designs are a totally different fit than other girls' clothing— they are a lot more comfortable. For example, the shorts are a little baggier but still sleek without being skintight. The sweatshirts are like men's but are roomier across the chest.

K&G: How did you get your idea off the ground?

First we went around the community and asked for help or sponsorships to get the clothing made. We found a lady who sewed. Since it was winter, the first designs were made out of fleece.

My mom helped a lot with marketing my clothing line. She faxed the story about how Pretty Tomboy was started to different magazines and newspapers that she thought might be interested. The newspaper here in Las Vegas was our first start. During our first year, my family and friends helped organize a talent show for Def Comedy Jam in California, where we modeled my designs and did a dance number. I also went to a convention in California that showcased the apparel of many different clothing designers. Through that experience, I met a lot of different people in the clothing industry. Basically, everything progressed from there. Magazines started contacting me for interviews. It was pretty overwhelming. I was like, "What's going on?" I had just gotten out of eighth grade!

K&G: What changes have you seen in your business from the time you started at age nine to today?
The clothing line has gone through a lot of changes. We've had a few people step in and try to help us create a bigger line, but because of my mom's health—my mom had a heart attack during our first year and was later diagnosed with lupus and diabetes—most of those efforts have had to be placed on the back burner.

Throughout the years, we have sold or given away different shirts, hats, pullovers, and other things. I would come up with new designs by looking at other clothing lines and thinking, "Why don't they have this?" "Why doesn't this t-shirt do all these different things?" "Why can't we have a fleece with four pockets in it?" I guess I just identified a need that was not being met. Last summer, when we were living in New Jersey, I did a lot of press. We had t-shirts made, we designed a lot of clothes, and we went to a lot of different companies with t-shirts, hats, and jackets—stuff like that—looking for a manufacturer and distribution channel. The complete clothing line hasn't totally materialized. We have still been pursuing it, but my sports and my mom's health take precedence.

Now, back in Las Vegas, we are selling some t-shirts and sweatshirts from our Web site as well as at my school;

however, I am really busy with school and sports, and my mom has been too ill to run it by herself. We would love to have someone step in and help us get a finished product line out, but because of our circumstances, we haven't been able to do it alone.

K&G: Who has helped you?
I'm so grateful to my mother and my family. They support me a lot. Other people, too, once they caught on to the concept. My friends think it's cool. They want me to keep going, keep trying. My best friend, Kayla, is there for me all the time.

K&G: What are you doing now?
I play soccer and basketball. My main sport right now is soccer, which I love. I love my team and my coach. In school I try hard and usually get at least one B, but this year I refuse to not get anything but straight As.

I plan to go to college to be a pediatrician. I'm really not into the sports thing past college. Sports are great, but I want to go to medical school.

K&G: How can other kids become clothing designers or own their own clothing lines?
Basically, you've got to start with your own thoughts and ideas. You've got to know your focus and always have the right people with you, like I had my mom. Then don't stop. Stick with it. I've been doing this for six years, which is a long time. You can't stop. I mean, it's not even close to being easy. It's not like snapping your fingers. So never stop—keep going.

K&G: What is your vision for your business and for your own life?
I want Pretty Tomboy Clothing to get off the ground, to leap and never fall back, for people to actually realize that it's a big thing. I want people to stop judging each other and just see each other for who they are.

K&G: Do you have a message for other kids?

The most important thing about Pretty Tomboy Clothing is my message to other girls: "Be yourself or please everyone else." I'm not going to change that. If you're not yourself, who are you? I mean, come on! I know that as you grow up you change, but you don't change for other people. Being something that you're not will not help make you who you want to be. Pretty Tomboy Clothing represents being true to who you want to be. I'm happy that I have a Web site where people can e-mail me and read about Pretty Tomboy Clothing and the events going on in my life. I'm also thankful for all the experiences I've had because of it.

Wrap-Up

Sometimes a dream comes from a life experience instead of a passion. Keisha didn't like being teased about her clothing choices and instead of letting it get her down, she turned a negative experience into a positive opportunity to create a dream.

Could you relate to Keisha's experiences? When searching for your dream, remember to look at your experiences as well as your passions. Your own personal experiences can provide the idea and motivation for a dream!

Contact Information

To reach Keisha, go to http://www.PrettyTomboy Clothing.com/.

CHAPTER 2

Believe

Before we go any further, let's talk about your beliefs. A belief is a concept or thought that you accept as true. We all have beliefs and they shape our reality. Your beliefs come from the thoughts you have about life that you've gathered through your experiences. These experiences and your environment determine what you accept as true about the world. Your beliefs guide your perceptions on your own potential for happiness and success. But be careful about basing your beliefs *solely* on what you have seen or have been told because this can limit your options and true potential.

For example, you might believe that everyone must go to college to be successful because you have been taught that this is true or because that is what your experiences have shown you to be true. But what about your friend who doesn't even consider going to college because his beliefs tell him that it is more important to follow in a family member's footsteps? Is it possible that he, too, can be successful? Of course he can.

Both beliefs arise from the different lives you have each lived. Each of us has his or her own beliefs, but they change as life experiences come and go. Ultimately it is up to you to decide what you want to believe in. No one can tell you what your beliefs should be.

What you believe in has a direct effect on what you will be able to accomplish. For example, ask yourself these questions: Do you believe that it is possible for you to live a life you dream of? Do you believe that you can accomplish your goals, no matter what obstacles come along? Do you believe that you have the strength and tenacity to achieve anything you set your mind to? The answers to these questions are important because if you want to succeed, you have to believe in yourself and your dream.

What if you have doubts? How can you change that? Let's start by taking a look at the phrase "believe in yourself." What does it really mean? It seems pretty simple, but let's break it down. To believe means to have *confidence* and *trust*; yourself means *everything that is you*—your strengths and your weaknesses, your fears and your dreams, your abilities, your gifts, your personality, your inspiration, your perception, your inner guidance, and your ability to make choices. Everything.

So "believe in yourself" means to have confidence and trust in all that is you. It means having confidence in who you are, your abilities, and who you project yourself to be. It means trusting in your gifts, talents, inner guidance, and, of course, your dreams. Think of it this way: Believing in yourself is like having your own personal kickstand. Wherever you go, you have something to lean on; without it, you fall down or have to depend on something else to keep you up.

If you don't really know who you are, what your talents are, and what makes you the person you are, believing in yourself can be more complicated. Let's try a quick exercise. ✐ Go to the back of the book and make a list of terms to describe yourself. Guides are there to help you focus on your strengths, your weaknesses, your specialties (things you know you are good at), your uniqueness (qualities that set you apart from everyone else), what you're good at, and words you would use to best describe yourself. Since it helps to get your thoughts on paper, write down the first things that come to mind when you look at each section. If you find that you're having negative thoughts about yourself, write them down, too. It is important to be honest with yourself about your true thoughts. If you acknowledge your negative thoughts, you can overcome them, but if you pretend they don't exist, they can undermine your efforts. Pay attention to how you feel as you are writing your list. After you're finished, come back to this spot in the book.

Did you learn anything about yourself? How did you feel when you were writing about yourself? You might have felt strong and empowered or embarrassed or shy, or maybe somewhere in-between. If someone else read what you wrote, would he or she gather that you have a lot of confidence about who you are, or that you lack confidence? Read your list out loud and pay attention to the image it conveys. Hopefully it's a positive one of you as an intelligent, creative, and valuable person—which is exactly who you are. If your list conveys a negative image, then you are focusing too much of your attention on negative thoughts or beliefs.

What can you do if you find that you have negative beliefs about yourself? Here's a quick trick that can help: *Change them.* Remember, they are only thoughts! In fact, these thoughts might not even be yours. You could be carrying around negative beliefs based on someone else's opinion of you. If anyone ever tries to convince you that you are anything less than amazing, don't fall for it! Each of us is a genius in his or her own way. We all have our strengths and we all have our weaknesses, but no matter who you are, you have the right to feel good about yourself. In fact, when you have a strong self-belief, people around you tend to believe in you as well. They follow your lead. Remember that. You can't hide what you believe about yourself because it is demonstrated in everything you do. People will believe in you as much as you believe in yourself!

Give this exercise a try to help shift your focus from the negative to the positive. Write down each negative thought on a piece of paper. Next to each negative thought write a positive thought that could replace it. Here's an example:

Negative belief: I can't do this; I don't know how.

Positive replacement: I *can* do this and what I don't know doesn't scare me. I can learn what to do or ask for help.

Do you see how this works? You can actually retrain your mind to think positively instead of negatively.

After you've written down your negative thoughts and their positive replacement thoughts, read them out loud. Notice the difference between what it feels like to think negatively and what it feels like to think positively. It not only *sounds* better when you're positive, but it also *feels* better to hear the positive thought versus the negative one. Any time you sense a negative thought creeping in, change it to a positive replacement. If you have to, carry your list with you to remind yourself of the new positive thoughts to focus on. Include a list of what you love about yourself that you can focus on as well. You will notice that your belief in yourself and your abilities grows stronger each time you choose to focus on something positive.

You may be wondering, "What does this have to do with my dream?" Belief in yourself comes into play when you are met with opposition, which may happen in the early stages of aspiring to live a dream. Most people who have lived a dream will tell you that there are always a few people (especially in the beginning) who try to discourage you. They may say things like, "That idea can't be done," "Someone your age certainly can't accomplish those goals," or "I know you and you don't have what it takes." It is during those times that you will need to rely on your belief in yourself. Everyone will have an opinion about what you are doing, but *your* own opinion must matter more than anyone else's. Hold on to your belief and never let it go. Put a stop to any opposition you might face by strengthening your belief in yourself.

What would you do if people tried to discourage you? Be ready for them so that they don't throw you off your game. Have enough belief in yourself that you can keep on going. You don't have to get into an argument about it; just walk away and refuse to allow their negative thoughts to affect you. Remember, *those* people aren't right about you unless you make them right about you. Your belief in yourself and your idea is the key to making all this work!

When you read our next interview with Leon Little, founder of Young Kids Against Violence, you'll see how far you can get when you truly believe in yourself and your dream.

LET'S DO IT!

Leon Little
Age 11
Clinton, Maryland

Founder of Young
Kids Against
Violence (YKAV),
Nonviolence activist,
Motivational speaker,
and Mentor

"Self-respect is the ultimate form of self-defense!"

Our setting for Leon's interview was in a park next to his grandmother's house. Although Leon is tall enough to be mistaken for a teenager and speaks with as much insight as an adult, he's just eleven years old. He has a peaceful quality about him. It was obvious, as we listened to his story, that creating peace was destined to be his path. Leon and his mom, Sherl, sat down with us. Sherl was very helpful in filling in details of Leon's early start in nonviolence activism, and it was evident that she is his strongest supporter. Leon was confident in his manner and is very committed to the cause of nonviolence. We were most impressed by his capacity to care for each individual's right to be safe from violence.

Meet Leon

Like any kid, Leon likes to play games, go to the park with friends, and play sports, but Leon is unique because he has created a dream from the simple belief that every person deserves to feel safe. By following his dream, Leon has accomplished many of his goals and brought about major changes in the world around him. As you get to know Leon, you will see that he loves to have fun even as he seriously campaigns for a society without violence.

K&G: Why did you become a nonviolence activist?

My dad is locked up on two life sentences, and my favorite uncle and cousin were fatally shot in two separate incidents. Nobody else should have to go through losing multiple family members to violence. I decided that in order for that to happen, I had to do something about it. My mom says you've got to be a part of the solution and not part of the problem, so I decided to make a difference by speaking out against violence. My school principal told me that I was just a little child and that my voice wasn't big enough to make a difference. His comments just motivated me to prove him wrong.

K&G: What did you do to become part of the solution?

Four years ago at age seven, I started Young Kids Against Violence, or YKAV. YKAV is a nonprofit peer group for peer mediation, nonviolence activism, and other programs. At that time, Congress was trying to pass a gun safety bill. I went to the Annapolis State House and Legislative Services Building to lobby for the bill. I wanted to get the people who opposed the gun safety bill to change their minds and pass it. My friends and I spoke with members of Congress, senators, and delegates. I also spoke at a hearing on gun safety with five of my friends. I said, "If my voice isn't loud enough to be heard, I will bring more of my friends next time." I got a call from the governor the next day; he told me that he'd heard my voice loud and clear!

The Responsible Gun Safety Act passed, and when it did my friends and I were excited to be invited by former president Clinton to witness Governor Parris N. Glendening sign the bill into law.

K&G: How did you start YKAV?

I first got in touch with some local police officers in the community to find a meeting space. After we negotiated a meeting space, I handed out flyers here and there. I carry flyers on me all the time. If I'm at a store, I stand outside to hand out flyers, talk to kids about joining YKAV, and network with adults.

We have two chapters. The one in Howard County has more than sixty members and the one in Prince George's County has about thirty or forty members. We meet at the Clinton police station. It's basically just word of mouth to get the message out to young kids that there's a club for them that's run by kids. It didn't take much funding to get started, and now we only need to raise money if we are having a big outreach program or event. I find that some sponsors want to help me but others won't because they think my program of nonviolence doesn't work.

When I wanted to start YKAV, people around me said, "There's no way you can reach out to these kids and stop them from fighting." I told them if I could keep the kids busy and not out on the streets, running around fighting, it would work. People still told me it wouldn't work because the kids would still want to fight, they would still want to buy the fighting games, and the games would still teach them to go out and beat up other kids. Whenever people would tell me that my idea wouldn't work, it would just motivate me to achieve my goals.

A lot of adults look at me like, "What are you doing? Violence is going to be here regardless of what you do." I say to them, "Well, if I can help one person and that one person helps one person and so on down the line, we'll build a link, and then a chain. And there won't be any violence within this chain." YKAV is here to let them know that we're not going to take the violence anymore.

K&G: What role do you play in YKAV?
As the founder, my individual role is the fix-it person or the problem solver. I'm very helpful and I don't like to [put anybody] down. I think that people should help and care for each other.

K&G: How does YKAV operate?
My cofounders, Jordan McGuill and Walter Richardson, run the club with me. The club is for kids and it's run by kids. We have a child board and an adult board. Both boards meet once a month, but when the adults meet, they talk about what the kids discussed the month before. Having both the adult and child boards creates a chain of communication, which is vital to our club's success.

We have outreaches at least once a month. An outreach is where we go out into the community and lend a helping hand, or throw a party, lock-in, or prom. Some of our outreaches are fun and some are what we call "reality checks" that help us learn life lessons. We speak out to the community to try to reach the younger kids, so when they get older, they won't get out on the streets and fight.

A lot of us mentor other kids. We'll usually have an activity during the week where we play basketball or do something fun with the kids we mentor. I mentor about eight or nine kids. My youngest mentee is three and my oldest mentee is fourteen. I'm a fun person so I can keep them busy. Sometimes I bring them to my house and we'll play on the computer or play a video game. Sometimes we'll go to the park and play football or basketball or just ride bikes around.

Recently, a senator challenged me by saying that I couldn't get people from different backgrounds together in one group for an extended period of time without having fights. So we had a youth lock-in with people from three different cities—Upper Marlboro, Clinton, and Greenbelt. We had more than three hundred kids show up from all different areas. We all spent the night together in a gymnasium. We had entertainment for the kids, and it was a lot of fun. Except for a few minor conflicts that were solved without violence, it all turned out very well.

At one of the "reality checks," [YKAV members and I] had a sleepover but the parents had it all set up so that [the] police were sent to the house. The police accused us of breaking a car window the night before. Even though a window hadn't really been broken, we were all blaming somebody different. [The group members and I] were handcuffed and put in a [jail] cell for two hours. It was just long enough to get the feel of "this is what happens when you break the law." None of us knew it wasn't for real, so we were pretty scared. We, the kids and adults associated with YKAV, feel that it is important to show the consequence of violence as well as spread the word of nonviolence. "Reality checks" give us a firsthand look at what happens when you choose a path of violence.

K&G: Who has helped you?

Some people who have played a major role in YKAV are my mom; my two cofounders and their parents; Miss Lisa Myers; and Corporal Frankenfield and many of the local police officers. The lieutenant governor and some of the people from the governor's board have also played important roles. The principal of my current school is very helpful to my club. Every once in a while he'll let me have an assembly for the school where I can speak out to the other kids. That really helps us get more members.

K&G: What role has the media played?

I got to be on the *Oprah Winfrey Show* through the Millennium Dreamers program. Disney and the McDonald's Corporation launched the program to find two thousand of the most extraordinary kids across the globe and honor their contributions to their communities. I was chosen as one of those two thousand kids, which was a big honor. Oprah picked twelve of us to be featured on her show; five got to be on the show in person and the other seven kids had videotaped interviews played during the show. I was one of the five picked to be on the show in person. I started getting more media attention after I was on *Oprah*. When people saw what had happened in my life, they wanted to do more for me. I would ask them not to do more for me but to do more to make sure that the kids who haven't yet had violence affect their lives never will.

Oprah was very nice. She helped me out a lot. She got the group Boyz II Men to sing "It's So Hard to Say Goodbye to Yesterday" via satellite. It meant a lot to me because the song was one of the things that helped motivate me to start YKAV. It came on the radio one day when my mom and I were driving down the road. I broke into tears because I missed my uncle and my cousin.

K&G: How has being a nonviolence activist affected your life?

Doing this work can be kind of hard. I sometimes get knocked around in school because I won't fight. A lot of kids know that I won't fight, so they try to take me on. A month before school ended another kid said that I did fight, even though I didn't. The end result was that we were both suspended.

People started treating me differently after I created YKAV. They see how much of a difference an eleven-year-old can make with his powerful voice. Many adults have started treating me with more respect and have started treating the eleven- and twelve-year-olds in our school with more respect.

K&G: What has been the most and least fun you have had throughout this experience?

What I like most is the media attention. When people see an eleven-year-old kid in the media, they want to know more about YKAV. The people who want to know more will go out and tell everybody else, and that will bring in more members, and more members means more fun.

The most fun I've had was during the YKAV's march in front of Wal-Mart. That was great because kids from all over the country came out to march with us. Our goal was to get kids off the street for that one day.

The thing that I probably like least is when people [put me] down, or when people say that since my father is locked up, I'm going to be locked up when I get older.

The scariest thing that I've done with YKAV is going to the Upper Marlboro Correctional Facility for one of our monthly outreaches. A guy [pretended to take] my shoes while I was locked up! It all ended up being a mock lock-up to teach us what it would feel like to be in a correctional facility, but we didn't know that at the time.

K&G: How can other kids become activists or start their own peer group?

If I want to do something and I don't know how to go about doing it, then the person I contact is the community police officer. I would suggest starting with your local police station or your local recreation center. Get involved with your community to see what people actually need. Don't listen to whoever puts you down. Just let what they say motivate you even more. My best advice is to never stop trying.

K&G: What is your vision for the future?

One of my personal goals is to attend Duke University, and then to be a professional NBA player and a pediatrician at the same time.

I am working on making a difference in my community. I want to turn my basement into a computer room to use in our mentor program. I've already gotten two companies to donate sixty computers.

One of the missions for YKAV was to be on the *Oprah Winfrey Show*. We've accomplished that, but our overall mission is for kids to be able to walk out of the house and not have to look over their shoulder and worry about who's behind them, ready to fight.

YKAV hasn't made a big impact yet, but hopefully we're on our way. I see some change in the kids who have joined our club, but a lot of kids are still getting into fights. What would make an impact is having more adult help, more adults here having fun with the kids, and more adult mentors. We are working toward setting up an adult mentor program, but a lot of adults say that they're too busy [to help out with young kids]. We'll keep trying, though.

K&G: Do you have a message for other kids?

YKAV has both a message and a motto. My general message is, "Self-respect is the ultimate form of self-defense," and YKAV's motto is adopted from a statement that I found on the Internet: *I will never bring a gun or a weapon to school. I will never use weapons or violence to settle a dispute. I will use my influence with my friends to keep them from using guns or weapons to settle disputes. My individual choices and actions, when multiplied by those of young people throughout the country, will make a difference.* Together, by honoring this pledge, we can reverse violence and grow up in safety.

Wrap-Up

Do you have a belief that is so strong that you have to do something about it? If you were to find other kids who believe in the same cause or idea, you could create a club or peer group, just like Leon did. Instead of being a victim, Leon chose to make a difference. Take your beliefs seriously and know that you, too, can make a difference in someone else's life, as well as in your own, just by following what you believe in.

Contact Information

If you would like to start a group like Leon's in your neighbor-hood, write to him and he'll give you some advice.

Leon Little
P.O. Box 24
Clinton, Maryland 20735

section 2

Inner Gifts

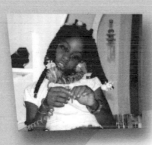

Inner Gifts

Who you are is your inner gift. You are a person with ideas, talents, messages, style, beliefs, and opinions. All these elements come together to make up your unique, authentic self. And it is from your unique, authentic self that your inner gifts are expressed.

Let's break it down: One essential element of your inner gift is having a unique talent or a natural ability to do something (or some things) very well. While some of these talents are external, such as playing the drums, painting, or putting things together, some talents are internal, such as being a natural leader, having an ability to learn new things quickly, or possessing a strong sense of compassion. These internal talents can also be considered pieces of your unique personality traits and may come so easily to you that you might not even be aware of them. On the other hand, your external talents might be uncovered when you explore activities you are drawn to. As you start to look for your talents, some will be easy to find and obvious, while others will need to be discovered and developed.

An equally important part of your inner gift is the unique way in which you express or convey your talents. Your expression is developed through your experiences, feelings, opinions, and perceptions of life. This unique expression can be translated through your individual style and through the overall message you convey. Your expression is a vital part of your gift because it is essentially what breathes life into your talents.

As an example, think of two of your favorite recording artists or athletes. What do you like about each of them? You'll probably find that you not only enjoy their singing or athletic talent but that you also connect with their style and personality, the messages in their songs, or their particular athletic technique. Even though two people might have similar talents (in this case, singing or sports), it is their expression of that talent that sets them apart. That's why no two people are exactly alike, and imagine how boring it would be if they were!

Your inner gift is one of a kind. Learning to tap into it can be very magical. Each component of your inner gift is like a puzzle piece: alone, each component is unique, but when connected to one another to form a whole, these gifts take on a shape—you! Your inner gift is unique and is intended to be used and shared with others. When you utilize your inner gift, it impacts and inspires those around you, helping to shape and form the world we live in. You can literally change the world by sharing your talents and openly expressing who you are. Just imagine the difference you can make!

In this section, discover the magic of your inner gift, learn how to support your gift and dream using your inner strength, and find out how to investigate helpful sources to make your dream a reality.

CHAPTER 3

Create

Now that you have identified the dream you want to work with and you have an understanding of your beliefs, let's take the process one step further!

First, let's do an exercise to get your creative juices flowing. As you might know, the left side of your brain manages the analytical side of living and the right side is in charge of the creative. So anytime you want to get your creativity flowing, do something that will stimulate the right side of your brain. For instance, take out a piece of scratch paper and create something on or with it. Something simple like doodling or drawing will do. If you like creative writing, write the first few sentences that come to you. If you enjoy making things, fold the piece of paper into a shape. Take two to five minutes for this exercise. The result doesn't have to be complete or perfect, but notice how doing something creative changes your focus.

Now that you have some creative energy flowing, it's time to use your imagination. Imagine a day living your dream. What would it look and feel like? Imagine that your dream could be everything that you want it to be and picture the most grandiose vision you can imagine. ✐ When the vision is complete, go to your chapter and write it all down. Be sure to include a lot of details.

Now that your picture is complete, let's explore the foundation of your dream.

✎ First, does your dream/idea incorporate your inner gifts? You may already be aware of the inner gifts you possess. If not, start by finding your unique talents. Look to subjects, areas, or hobbies that spark a strong interest in you as you look to uncover your unique talents. Also, think of abilities that come very easily to you. For example, you might find it easy to make people laugh or be a strong leader, you might naturally have a great singing voice or an ability to build things, or it might be natural for you to invent things or communicate with others. Your special talents could be right under your nose, but if you have any problems finding them, ask people close to you what they think you are naturally good at. Sometimes it is easier for other people to see what you cannot.

If you would like more examples of what a natural talent or personal expression might be, pay close attention to the interviews in this book. Each kid we interviewed has his or her own unique talent and message to convey. Just as this became evident to us as we learned more about these young people, your talents and personal expression will be revealed to you as you continue to learn more about yourself.

✎ Once you find your talents or interests, explore them. Figure out what you like and what you don't like. Be yourself and be willing to express yourself fully and honestly. Share your unique personality and talent with others. This is how you will best uncover all your inner gifts. Your special talents and the way in which you express them are part of what makes you the person you are. When you build your dream around your inner gifts, you give a voice to the essence of who you are. You express your true self, and that is what will make you feel good about yourself and your dream. ✎ Take a minute now to go to your chapter and write down the inner gifts your dream is built around.

Some people have a dream of becoming rich and famous. Be careful not to make this your entire focus. It's fine if having money and fame is one of the results of following your dream, but you will want to keep your focus on being the best at what comes naturally to you and follow your desire to express yourself. Focus on feeling great by choosing to do what inspires you, instead of on the results it might bring.

Next, let's define the purpose of your idea. What is your reason for pursuing the idea or dream you have chosen? For example, if you want to start a group to collect trash on the beach, your purpose might be to have clean, safe beaches. If you come up with more than one purpose, that's OK; dreams may often have more than just one. Having a purpose really helps you maintain your focus throughout the process of creating your dream. ✎ Take a minute to write down your purpose.

Last but not least, what is the motivation behind your idea? Motivation is different from purpose because it is the feeling that fuels your desire to strive for your dream. Your motivation could be that your dream or idea is something you love to do, fulfills a need you have, or sounds like a lot of fun. Using the beach cleanup example again, one possible motivation could be that this type of project would make you feel good because you would be protecting the environment. Be honest with yourself about what your motivation is. It will help you understand more about who you are and what is important to you. It can also indicate how successful you will be in pursuing your dream.

If your motivations come from other people's desires or from outside influences, you might want to think twice before pursuing this dream. Doing something simply because someone else wants you to, because it looks good, or because it increases your status with your friends places your motivation outside of yourself. If this happens, you aren't in control of that motivation and it may leave you feeling that you haven't been true to your own gifts and talents. You also won't have the passion and energy you need to keep going and might run out of steam before your project is complete. Be sure to have your own motivation before following any idea or dream. ✎ Turn to your chapter and write down your motivation.

Now that you have your dream well defined, what will you need to make it happen? ✎ Start a list of necessary supplies and any costs associated with them. If you feel that you need advice because you aren't quite sure what you'll need, where to start, how to do something, or where to get the information you need, make of list of these questions. You can find answers in lots of places; friends, parents and other adults, books, and the Internet are just a few examples. Do you need a pair of extra hands or an extra brain to help you out? If so, list how many people you think you might need. Do you need a place to sell a product or gather a group? No matter how big or little your needs are, put them down in writing.

The reason it is important to ask yourself these questions and to make lists is to help you get organized, identify what you want your dream to be, and give you a good idea of how to go about achieving it. Putting your ideas down on paper helps you see what you have and what you need in order to realize your dream.

In the next interview, read how B.J. Pinchbeck, a webmaster, turned his dream into a reality by using his passion for computers as his motivation for creating an informational homework helper Web site.

LET'S DO IT!

B.J. Pinchbeck
Age 15
pittsburgh,
pennsylvania

webmaster and
creator of B.J.
pinchbeck's
Homework Helper

"Be determined. Don't stop."

We met B.J. and his older sister, Megan, at her apartment, where B.J. was staying for a couple of weeks during summer break. B.J. and Megan have a great relationship. Their playful connection helped break the ice for any interview jitters. And when the two of them wanted to see if we were really traveling in an RV, it was fun to take them on a tour of our wheeled home.

Meet B.J.

B.J. didn't start out intending to create the first and largest homework helper Web site on the Internet. His intention was to create a project that he and his dad could do together for fun. B.J. and his dad created a Web site that other kids could use, too. As a result, at the age of nine, B.J. became a webmaster. B.J. is very knowledgeable about Web design and computer programming. He even offered us a few pointers for our own Web site!

K&G: Why did you create a homework helper Web site?

It all happened kind of by accident. Not long after my dad and I started using the Internet, we began searching for

Web sites to help me with my homework. During our searches, we discovered that there were not a lot of good sites that had educational or homework help links. We found it frustrating to have to keep bookmarking all the educational sites. We decided to try making a Web site that had all the good homework links that we had found. We downloaded some Web-making software [an HTML editor], and, just for fun, we tried it out and found that it wasn't all that hard to make a Web page.

K&G: What was involved in turning your original idea into a Web site?

First we found a Web site that helped us learn how to do HTML, which is the computer language that most Web sites are built with. Then we bought a Web-editing program and started out by making the site very basic with only a few links—maybe a hundred or so. We kept adding links as we got into it.

The initial cost to start the site was nothing. We got the Web site for free through our local e-mail server. Once we got our domain name, BJPinchbeck.com, we had to pay thirty dollars a month, but by that time we had sponsors to help with the cost.

We acquired our links by scanning the Internet. After we had a pretty sizeable list of links, we just kept editing them. Eventually we added new sections and subtitles to help direct the kids to what they needed to find. Right now we have about 750 links.

The end product is a homework helper site that helps you categorize your homework and shows you where you can find the information you need. The site can help students of any age, from preschool to college.

The most unique qualities about our site are that it was one of the first homework helper sites out there and that it is co-run by a kid.

K&G: How did B.J. Pinchbeck's Homework Helper continue to grow?

When we started out we just wanted the site to be like a little fun project that my dad and I would do. Then it started getting in the local newspapers. After that, we started getting really excited about it, so we kept getting further and further into it, and it just kept getting bigger and bigger. I received a lot of help and encouragement from my dad to make it all happen.

At one point we found schools and whole school districts that are listed on the Web and sent a letter to principals or to technical coordinators, notifying them of our site. That's how the publicity started. If you get into a teaching environment, information goes down the hallway from one teacher to another. Then their students learn about it. The Internet can be a fast way to get the word out!

At first we had around twenty visitors a day, but half of them were probably us. Gradually we started to see that number grow as the Web site got popular in the community. We started getting letters from everyone who had heard about it. Eventually we saw it grow to hundreds and thousands of visits to the site. Now it's around 10,000 visitors a day. The biggest thing that's happened to our site was the partnership with the Discovery Channel School. Discovery Channel read about us in the *New York Times* and decided to make a student section on its site, DiscoverySchool.com. So we went down to their offices and talked to them, and the rest is history. We thought it was great!

K&G: What role do you play in BJPinchbeck.com?

My individual role is getting and checking the links—they will go down sometimes—answering e-mails, and performing miscellaneous maintenance to the Web site. I would like to add some Flash animations to the site. Now that DiscoverySchool.com has partnered with us, we don't do as much of the designs as we did before because they have staff dedicated to designing its Web site.

K&G: Do you receive e-mail from kids?

Currently we receive about thirty e-mails a day, depending on the time of year. The questions we receive range from needing help for projects and kids wanting SAT cheat sheets to questions on five-page projects that are due the next day. We also receive questions from little kids.

The kids really do talk to us, unlike some other sites where they stay away from corresponding with the people. We respond by giving them links to their answers. We don't give them the answers; we guide them to the right places to find the information.

K&G: What has been the most and least fun you have had throughout this experience?

What I like the most about being a webmaster are the e-mails I receive from the kids. I love seeing their personalities come out and I love to hear how excited they are when they get my replies. What I like the least is checking the links. It is a never-ending job. Once you get it done, you have to do it again.

K&G: How can other kids create a successful Web site?

Start with the basics and then work up. You can't expect to make a gigantic Web site like Amazon.com or something on the first day. Keep it simple and do some planning. This will help you avoid a lot of mistakes. We didn't do much planning up front, but once we got started we realized it's important.

If you want to use software to build a Web site, I would try using FrontPage or DreamWeaver, but they can be expensive. Any of the Macromedia software is good. HoTMetal is good, too. There are also free programs on the Internet that can help you start your Web site. Think big, but start small. Don't get caught up in adding more advanced elements until you've gotten the hang of basic Web site design. Then follow through with it. Be determined and don't stop!

K&G: What is your vision for the future?

My dream is to become a computer programmer and maybe go to Carnegie Mellon University. During the summer I teach a week-long course with my dad at Penn State for junior webmasters who want to learn how to do Web design. The course is on DreamWeaver, Flash, and Fireworks.

Wrap-Up

B.J. used his inner gifts to guide him to develop a particular type of project: a Web site that helps other kids. He didn't start out by saying, "Computer programming is one of my inner gifts, so I think I will create a Web site." Instead, he worked at what felt good and, in doing that, found a purpose for his talents. B.J.'s dream filled a need that others had and created a project that was fun for his dad and him. Look at your everyday life. Could you create a project (even a Web site) using your inner gifts?

Contact Information

To reach B.J., go to http://www.BJPinchbeck.com.

CHAPTER 4

Inner Strength

What do you think it means to have inner strength? Outer strengths are easy to define because they are visible qualities, such as physical power, agility, coordination, and talent. But internal strength isn't something you can see or touch. What do you think are some characteristics of inner strength?

To help you identify these qualities, it might help you to have an example. Think of someone who you believe has a lot of inner strength. Got that person in mind? Great; now answer the following questions in your head:

- Does this person have the courage to be an original, to do things his or her own way?

- Does this person know that his or her life goals can be accomplished?

- Does this person stand up for him- or herself when it is necessary?

- Does this person refuse to allow other people's opinions to affect his or her success?

- Does this person keep striving for new goals?

- Does this person know that he or she can depend on him- or herself when times get tough?

You probably answered "yes" to most or all these questions. These questions contain examples of what it means to have inner strength, and they revolve around qualities such as courage, endurance, tenacity, patience, and the willing-ness to push forward in the face of opposition. If you had to ask yourself these questions, how do you think you would answer? ✍ Take a few minutes and give it a try. Answer honestly.

How did you do? Did you still answer "yes" to all the questions? If you did, you've already found ways to recognize and tap into your inner strength. If you answered "no" to many of the questions, you may feel that you lack inner strength. Achieving your dream requires inner strength, but don't worry! You do have it! All you have to do is learn how to tap into it.

Here are some ideas to help you:

- Be willing to be an original. Draw from your own creativity and do things the way you want to do them. Most of the world's important and influential ideas came about because someone took a risk and decided to be an original; it shows a lot of inner strength to put new ideas out there.

- Know that you can do anything you wish in life. It might take a little work, but you can achieve anything you want.

- Communicate your desires and opinions the way you want. Find your voice and have the confidence to use it, whether things are going well or not. This is your project; speak up and be heard!

- Be your biggest supporter. Some people might like your project while others might not. You can't please everyone. Reacting to other people's opinions could make you feel as if you're on an emotional rollercoaster: you're happy when people love your work, but you feel down when they don't. Your goal is to achieve a constant satisfaction with your progress that is not swayed by outside opinion. If you only get excited about your project when people like it, you allow outside forces to help you create it and affect your choices. Find pride in your work so that you won't be tempted to seek out others' approval.

● Keep striving to achieve new goals. If you want to move in another direction or set your goals higher than you have before, then do it! Keep aiming higher and reassess your goals often.

● Congratulate yourself for your small successes along the way. From time to time, take a step back and recognize all that you have accomplished. It's OK to give yourself a pat on the back!

● Have the courage to keep going, keep following your dreams, and never give up.

Inner strength is about not giving up when things get bad and knowing you have what it takes to move past any obstacle. When you have inner strength you are able to move forward even if something unexpected happens, and you can acknowledge that you have the abilities and talents to achieve anything you wish.

✍ What are some examples of ways you have used your inner strength? Imagine meeting someone who doesn't like your idea and tells you that you should just throw in the towel. What are some ideas you have about using your inner strength to get by this obstacle? Share your thoughts in your chapter. If you need some help getting started, perhaps the following interview with motivational speaker Precious Thomas will inspire you.

LET'S DO IT!

Precious Thomas
Age 10
Suitland, Maryland

Motivational speaker

"To know me is to love me."

We met Precious and her adopted mom, Rocky, in a private banquet room at B. Smith's Restaurant in Washington, D.C., where Precious was the evening's keynote speaker. Precious, a little girl dressed in pink, her favorite color, sat at the head of the table. Twenty adults filled the rest of the table, waiting eagerly to hear her story and message.

Precious has been giving speeches and reciting poems to public audiences since she was two years old. That night the audience was captivated by Precious's speech. All were quite eager to ask her questions about her life, her poetry, and her disease. After we listened to her speech and the follow-up questions from her audience, we were just as eager to talk to Precious one-on-one.

Meet Precious
Precious, the daughter of a drug-addicted birth mother, was born infected with HIV. She has used her incredible life's story to speak to groups about her message of hope, awareness, kindness, and the importance of HIV and AIDS prevention. Precious has always had a knack for memorization. This gift has helped her become a powerful motivational speaker at a very early age.

K&G: How did you become a motivational speaker?

I started speaking when I was two years old. A friend of my mom's, who worked at a radio station, heard me speak and knew that there was something special about the way I spoke and how much I could remember at such a young age. She told my mom that she wanted to put me on the radio. My mom agreed, and I have been speaking to groups ever since. When I first started speaking in public I would recite Maya Angelou's poems, the Lord's Prayer, and the Apostles' Creed. I gave my first speech at the AIDS Walk at Greater Mount Calvary Church here in Maryland. People started hearing about me, and I was asked to speak at different events, at places like schools, churches, and other functions. My main intention when I speak is to educate people about HIV and AIDS.

K&G: How do you prepare for your speaking events?

Now that I attend boarding school, I speak one or two times a month. I prepare my speeches by writing down the experiences that I have been through in my life. Then I write down what I would like to say and how I want to say it. My speeches change from group to group. I write all my own speeches and get help on some of my poems. My message is about HIV and AIDS awareness, but from the way that I start my speeches, you wouldn't know that HIV is the topic I'm going to speak about.

K&G: How do people find out about you as a motivational speaker?

People find out about me through newspaper articles, radio stations, television stations, and magazine stories. Right now my attorney makes the arrangements for my speaking engagements.

K&G: Who has helped you?

I receive a lot of encouragement from my mother, my doctor, my teachers, and my preacher. They help me stay strong, [help me] not give up, and [help me] take all my medicine.

K&G: Who is your typical audience?

I often speak to kids my own age or kids twelve years old and older. I used to speak mostly for adult groups because most schools don't allow people to talk about stuff like HIV or AIDS until the kids in the audience are older. I educate the adults so that the adults can educate the children.

I speak all over the country. The groups I speak to include companies, schools, colleges, universities, churches, business groups, birthday groups, youth organizations, and even the [former] president of the United States, Bill Clinton. I am also an ambassador for Camp Heartland. Camp Heartland is a camp for kids who have been impacted by HIV or AIDS. It is a place they can go to for a week and have the best time of their lives.

K&G: What has been the most fun you have had throughout your speaking experience?

My favorite thing is to know that I have reached someone through my speaking. My most memorable moment was a concert given for me by my church. The guest was a gospel singer named Vickie Winans.

K&G: What has been the least fun you have had throughout your speaking experience?

The hardest thing about being a motivational speaker is being teased by people who have not been educated about HIV and AIDS.

K&G: How can other kids become motivational speakers?

Start by speaking at home with your family and friends. Believe what is in your heart. It's like a secret that is so hard to keep that you may as well talk about it. You never know what the reaction is going to be. Stay strong. You should follow your dream and go through with it if that's what you want to do. It just might work out for you. Go for your dream and don't let anybody stop you.

K&G: What are your visions for the future?

A couple of goals that I have are to graduate from high school with all passing grades at the age of fifteen and then go to college. I am two grades ahead of other kids my age in school. I am not yet sure what I would like to go to college for, but I do know that I would like to be able to go.

K&G: Do you have a message for other kids?

My message to others is that although I might not look sick or be sick, you don't have to look sick or be sick to have HIV or AIDS. I would like my audience to walk away from my speeches knowing that they should be friends to people with HIV or AIDS and not be afraid of them. Something that I would want people to know about me is that I am a beautiful, proud African American. I also have messages in the poems I write, like in my poem entitled "Who am I?"

Who am I?
I am a child whose inner child wants to be loved, have fun, and
*   be well.*
I am your mother, maybe your father, perhaps your sister,
*   possibly your brother.*
I am sky and I am earth, an important part of this universe.
A hug and a smile, what things could be worse?
I am not poison, danger, death, or disease.
I am a friend, my life's not at ease.
He is she and she is he
And we are us so don't sit there and look with disgust.

Who am I, you dare to say?
Well, I am me, still alive as can be.
And one of these days when I am gone
And life continues to carry on

Remember me always.
Remember me well.
Remember my life so you can tell
Just who I am, for I will always be

whether a bird, a flower, grass or a tree,
I will forever always be me.

Wrap-Up

Sometimes your own life can be the source of your inner strength. Precious has been able to use the story of her life to help others. Her message of tolerance, friendship, and love inspires others every day. Precious says, "To know me is to love me," and "Be a friend, not afraid." It takes inner strength to look past other people's judgments of you and ask them to be your friend.

What inner strengths do you possess? Your life experiences may be vastly different from Precious's, but they might be similar in terms of being strong against adversity, learning to overcome hardships, and helping to pass along a message of tolerance, friendship, and love.

Contact Information

To reach Precious, contact her at:

Precious Thomas
C/O Rocky Thomas
P.O. Box 722
Suitland, MD 20746

CHAPTER 5

Investigate

Inquiry, also known as the process of asking questions, is a necessary step toward moving your dream from idea to action. At this point, it's important to know that asking lots of questions is an excellent way to approach any project. It doesn't mean you are ignorant or naïve; it means that you care enough about your dream to get the best information from the best sources. For example, if you are interested in building a Web site and you want to know which software is the best, you wouldn't call up the local plumber for advice; you would want to talk to someone with Web and computer experience. The best way to get helpful information is to speak with people with experience and knowledge about the subject in question. Prepare some questions ahead of time. You might come up with more questions during your meeting, but have a strong foundation to start from.

✍ Coming up with questions to get the information you need doesn't have to be intimidating. You already have a great place to start: read over the list of needed supplies, resources, and information that you created in chapter 3. If you need supplies, ask yourself where you might be able to find or obtain them. If you don't know where to go, then that's a great question to ask someone with experience related to your idea. Going back to the Web site example, you may know that you need software and you may even know exactly which software you want, but do you know where to get it for the best price? Do some research by calling local software merchants and asking for prices.

Search the Internet for what you want. Ask someone with computer expertise where the best places to buy software are.

✑ Start a list of your possible resources. There are some guides in your chapter to help you. Come up with as many ideas as you can. Include any guesses you might have about where you could obtain information about the items on your list. Remember to include a list of people who can help you obtain what you need or who can share ideas with you on where to look for answers. People are a great resource and most people are happy to help you. Remember that there is no wrong way to ask a question. The more you practice asking questions, the better you will be at knowing what works and the stronger your confidence in your ability to inquire.

Here are some resource ideas to assist you in your search:

- Check the back of this book. Chapter 14 is dedicated to resources that can help you find what you need.

- Ask around at your school. Teachers, counselors, librarians, and other faculty members might have some great information for you.

- Look for community resources. The Small Business Administration or the chamber of commerce helps people with their ideas. Some communities may even offer classes or counseling for projects like yours.

- Visit your local library. Look for books or magazines that have information that can help you. If you need assistance, the librarians are extremely knowledgeable.

- Research people or companies that have had experience doing something similar to what you want to do. Use their paths as models for ways you can go about accomplishing your own dream.

- Find people or companies with experience related to your idea and ask them for an interview. Find out how they got started, where they went for help, and what obstacles or successes they may have encountered. They will probably have helpful resources for you as well.

● Ask family members or friends if they know of anything that can help you.

● Look on the Internet. If you don't have access to it at home, you can use it at your local library. The Internet has an incredible amount of helpful information for any idea or dream.

Here are some helpful tips when using the Internet:

● Use multiple keywords or key phrases instead of only one keyword to help narrow your search.

● Try using different search engines, including those that specialize in helping young people.

● Look up companies, groups, or organizations that help young people, like Boys and Girls Clubs or local community centers.

Keep asking lots of questions. The information you need is out there and there are people who will support and help you. All you have to do is connect with them. Remember, even if you are uncertain of how to move forward or if you are around people who don't seem to be supporting you and your dreams, help is out there. Just keep searching!

Be confident and ask for what you need. You're more likely to get what you want if you ask for it. It's that simple. You may not get what you ask for every time, but what are your chances of getting anything if you never ask at all?

Start putting some action into your dream. Once you have done some research you will start to get an idea of what it takes to move forward. You won't be able to anticipate everything that you will need, but as your idea grows and starts to take form, keep adding to the list of needed supplies. Be sure to cross off the items you obtain or that you decide aren't necessary.

✍ If you need help staying inspired and focused, find and read stories about people who inspire you. Look at people who started with nothing and still created amazing things. Use them as models for your success. What did they do? How did they become successful? What was their daily inspiration? Who is someone you would like to research who might inspire you? There are so many success stories out there. If other people can find and live their dreams, you can do it, too! The following interview with Jeremy Valdes, founder of REACT (Reforming Education Around Our Communities' Troubles) proves it.

LET'S DO IT!

Jeremy Valdes

Age 15
Tampa, florida

founder of
REACT

"Anything is possible!"

During Jeremy's interview we were surrounded by his family members in their home in Tampa, Florida. Jeremy and his mom, dad, and two younger sisters greeted us at the front door. It was one of our first interviews, so we were nervous. Jeremy's friendly family put us at ease right away. We could see how much his family has played an important role in his life. As the interview progressed we learned how the family's support has been a key element to

Jeremy's success. His family has been there to help with ideas, lend a hand, and give advice.

Meet Jeremy

After attending a school assembly where motivational speakers talked to students about doing something positive in their schools and communities, Jeremy walked away with more questions than answers. He also walked away with an idea. Jeremy sought out the people who could answer his questions and help him make his idea a reality. He developed a program that allows kids to share with one another their observations about their community's troubles and their possible solutions to them. REACT (Reforming Education Around Our Communities' Troubles) helps to establish an open line of communication and an overall atmosphere of cooperation between students and adults. With the help of his group, Jeremy teaches other kids to react to problems proactively by asking questions and participating in problem-solving activities.

K&G: Why did you start your project?

I started REACT in the eighth grade after attending an assembly at school where we learned how people could do something positive in their schools and communities. After that, I started looking at our community and school troubles more closely.

What really motivated me was thinking about all the bad things that happen and hearing about what happened at Columbine High School and other places. It made me think that if this kind of thing happens in schools, it has to be happening in the community. So I thought I could create a program [that focused on] community outreach programs and projects. We could try working from within the school to prevent those things from happening in the community.

K&G: What was involved in starting REACT?

I started by speaking with the human relations specialist at my school. She suggested an idea that a couple of students and I could expand on and told us that she would get all the paper-work done if we could get the program set up. So with our initial five people, we started REACT.

K&G: How does REACT operate?
We find problems in our community that need solving and use them as topics to focus on. We also look at needs in our school that aren't being met. First we chose cooperation. We thought that was a big thing that was missing. Then we chose teamwork. Teamwork and cooperation were both needed and they go hand in hand. To be a team is to accomplish something together and to cooperate is to work together to get something done more eas-ily and more quickly. [In order for REACT to be effective in its mission, we had to make sure that as a group, we were willing to work as a team and cooperate.]

For the rest of my eighth grade year, REACT focused on team-work and cooperation. The principal granted me permission to have meeting periods during homeroom, so we met every morning and worked on creating various activities for our school's students that would be good to build teamwork. [Such activities may have involved both physical and intellectual challenges, like tugs-of-war and group problem-solving ses-sions. The activities were based on the process of teamwork, and they were meant to help kids understand the importance of working together and didn't necessarily focus on any one specific topic.] The activities we created were fun but also taught a lesson. They were held on one of our school's Jour-ney Days. Journey Days are special events that the school plans for one day, once every two weeks. In honor of our program, the school gave us a Journey Day to platform our activities. It was called REACT Day.

K&G: How is the project funded?
To help fund the project, Miss Hollinger, the human rela-tions specialist, and I put in applications for grants. I received a $1,300 Peacemaker Award, sponsored by the University of South Florida's School of Psychology. This

grant is given to students whose projects help their schools and communities become safer places.

K&G: Where are you now with the project?

Now I'm in high school and am trying to get REACT set up there. To get it set up and to get the funding, I have to go through the officers of student government. They control the school's finances. I've already given the officers and my principal the proposal to start the REACT program. Once I get support for the program, then funding will be needed. If I keep persisting, I have about a 95 percent chance of getting the program started in my high school, just like I did in my middle school.

K&G: What has been the most fun you have had throughout this experience?

The most fun I've had is getting the Peacemaker Award from the University of South Florida [USF] for starting REACT in my middle school. It was really fun. I met the USF athletic director, Lee Roy Selmon, and the president of the university, Judy Genshaft, plus a lot of other people. I was the only one who won an individual award; the rest of the awardees were groups. The winners and their families were treated to a USF game, which was really fun.

K&G: How can other kids start a school project?

You've got to always know that anything's possible. It's really easy if you just set your mind to it. Get into the politics of your school. If you are involved in school politics, your voice will have a greater chance of being heard. I'm the sophomore class president, and I'm involved in other clubs and school organizations. It all helps my voice be heard and gives me practice speaking in front of groups of people. This kind of practice will help you look more professional when you have to stand up in front of a big crowd and get your program up and going.

Try to do well in school. I know it's been preached and preached and that both teachers and your parents say,

"You've got to stay in school," but it's also really important to try to do well. My advice is to sit down with your parents and talk to them. Your parents are your biggest supporters and your biggest fans, and they are there for you through thick and thin. They'll help you out with anything you need. My mom and dad helped me out a lot. They gave me the inspiration. They just told me, "You can do whatever you want. You can do anything if you put your mind to it."

K&G: What is your vision for the future?

I would like to get REACT up and going in my high school. I hope that it catches on with the school superintendent and spreads through all the schools. Once I have it running, I plan on doing it through high school. When I go to college I'll leave the program in somebody else's hands. That way I can just focus on college. My dream is to accomplish a lot of things when I'm finished with college and to try to have an influence on the world. I'd like to spread my message that anything is possible if you just put your mind to it. I would like to be a lawyer or a psychologist, or combine the two—law and psychology—and deal with criminal psychology.

Wrap-Up

Jeremy knew that if he wanted answers to his questions, he needed to ask for help. And with the help he received, Jeremy realized that he could make a difference by getting involved in his school and community.

Do you have unanswered questions? Have you had an idea but could not make it work? Seek out others, maybe your parents, teachers, or even counselors in your school, to help you answer your questions. Like Jeremy, don't be afraid to ask for help.

Contact Information

To reach Jeremy, e-mail him at jeremy@planetgiggle.com.

section 3

Passion

Passion

You may have heard the phrase "follow your passion." Passion is the excitement, motivation, and drive you feel to follow a dream. Some call it your heart's desire. Others call it your inspiration. The way you know if you are following the passion in your dream is by how you feel when you are doing it. Doing things you love brings out your passion.

To find your passion, experiment with exploring your interests, doing things you're good at, and engaging in creative activities. Pay attention to how these activities make you feel. When you find something that makes you feel enthusiastic, inspired, and as if you never want to stop, that is how you know you have found your passion. When it comes time to choose a dream or even a path in life, choose one that makes you feel that excitement, motivation, and drive. When you do, the world responds to you with the same enthusiasm and will open up in ways you can't even imagine!

In this section, support your passion by investing in yourself and your idea, find the confidence to let others see your dream, and become inspired by your ideas.

CHAPTER 6

Invest in Yourself

Investing in yourself means committing to your project, setting goals, taking responsibility for your choices and outcomes, having integrity, and respecting yourself, your ideas, and others along the way.

To start investing in yourself, first commit yourself to your idea or project. Commitment shows how much you believe in it and how serious you are. Now that you are getting started, it's time to roll up your sleeves and get busy. Be advised: you may have to do some things that you don't really want to do. It's all part of being invested in your project. Once you commit yourself to your dream, go for it and never look back!

Have integrity with yourself, your project, and the people you work with. If you say you will do something, then do it. Making excuses for not keeping promises or honoring commitments disrespects the people you are working with as well as the project. If you don't think a situation will work, be honest with the people involved. Confront issues, even tough ones, up front so that you can move forward. The people you're working with would rather know the truth right away than be left wondering. Avoiding issues can appear dishonest. Your idea's success will depend on other people's willingness to work with you. Your integrity, honesty, and ability to follow promises with action will allow others to feel that they are being treated fairly. In return, they will treat you fairly.

You never know who you will need to count on, so be respectful, courteous, and grateful to everyone along your path. This is easy; just treat people with respect and kindness and make it a point to let them know how much you appreciate them. Hey, this includes you, too! Treating yourself with respect and kindness teaches others to treat you with respect and kindness as well.

🖎 Set goals to help you stay focused and give you direction. One great result of setting goals is that you can use them to measure the success of your efforts. Here are some simple guidelines to use when setting goals for yourself:

● Set both short-term and long-term goals. Both are valuable. Setting short-term goals gives you small accomplishments to celebrate along the way to fulfilling your long-term goals, and they are important motivators to help keep you moving forward.

● Setting both personal and professional goals helps move you toward accomplishing your dreams. Here are some tips:

■ Create goals that reflect what you want to accomplish.

■ Create goals that will help you perform better.

■ Create goals that are important to you, not goals that some-one else wants for you or goals that just sound good.

■ Include details in your goals.

■ State your goals in positive terms instead of negative ones. Always keep your focus on the positive (e.g., "I would like to learn how to draw faces more accurately" instead of "I would like to stop making mistakes when drawing faces.").

■ Make your goals realistic and measurable by creating a timeline. Ask yourself, "When do I want to have certain things done by?" Be sure to give yourself enough time to complete your task and state it in terms that specify a deadline so that you can identify when it has to be accomplished by (e.g., "Research five different product costs by 5:00 PM Friday, August 1" instead of "Research product costs").

■ Set up a system of accountability by establishing guidelines for what will happen if you do or do not meet your goal. Give yourself rewards for meeting your goals and consequences for not. Find someone to help you make yourself accountable for those rewards and consequences.

■ Reassess your goals often and allow your goals to change and grow with your project.

■ Remember to use the visualization techniques you learn in this book. Keep visualizing yourself achieving your goal.

■ ✍ Create a goal collage to make your goal setting fun. Find pictures and phrases that represent your goals and paste them in your chapter or on poster board or tack them to a corkboard.

✍ Now it's time to try it for yourself! Get started by coming up with steps and actions that you will need to take in order to see your project succeed and give yourself a time to have it finished by. There are examples in your chapter to help you begin. Set as many goals as you can. Be sure to set short- and long-term goals and be realistic about the timeline.

Investing in both yourself and your idea brings strength, confidence, and momentum to your project. Can you feel the excitement and momentum for your idea building? Let's keep going!

Here are some additional ideas to consider:

● Immerse yourself in your dream. Surround yourself with people, materials, and books that build on your idea. Make your dream a part of your daily life.

● Find classes, join a club, or sign up for an internship that can help to expand your knowledge about your field or a related field.

● Continue to learn new concepts and new ways to approach situations. Read about, research, and practice your skills. Find ways to broaden your experience as well as your knowledge.

● Give yourself time for the things that are important to you; this includes personal time just for you. Even Justin Miller, whose interview follows, has to take time off from being the World's Youngest Chef every now and then.

LET'S DO IT!

Justin Miller
Age 12
pittsburgh,
pennsylvania

world's
youngest chef

"Just go for it! It's a lot of fun!"

Justin's interview was at his grandparents' home, where we were welcomed as though we were members of the family. Justin's grandparents were very proud of him and his accomplishments. Before the interview, Justin's dad, Jimi, played some videos of Justin's TV interviews. Justin has been receiving media attention since a very young age; some of the interviews and national talk show appearances started when he was just five years old. We all laughed as we watched Justin, as a small child, make the audience and host laugh without even trying. We had a great time watching Justin's interviews. His commitment to learning everything about his craft and his passion for the art of cooking was amazing.

Meet Justin

You could say Justin was born to be a chef. He grew up cooking. Before he reached middle school, Justin had written two cookbooks, been a guest on numerous talk shows, and had been inducted into the *Guinness Book of World Records* in 2003 as the World's Youngest Chef. Justin has accomplished more than some people three times his age, and he's only getting started!

K&G: How did your passion for cooking begin?

When I was really young I would pull out pots and pans—not to bang on them but to pour things into them. When I was almost two years old, my mom and dad worked with me hand-over-hand to teach me about cooking. They would let me put my hand on the mixer, and they would put their hand over mine to control it. I enjoyed cooking so much that they couldn't keep me out of the kitchen.

The first thing I ever made were cabbage rolls. I was only eighteen months old at the time. My father suggested to my mom, "Why don't you give him the cabbage leaf and the meat and stuff and see what he does?" So I looked at mine, I looked back at my mother's, then I rolled mine up like hers. That's when I knew that cooking was what I wanted to do with my life.

K&G: Who has helped you?

My parents always made sure that the kitchen was safe for me. They reorganized the cupboards to keep unsafe items out of my reach, and they also supervised my cooking. I received a lot of support from my family, including my grandparents. They didn't push me into it; they let me make up my own mind.

K&G: How did cooking with your mom develop into a career as a chef?

I had always watched my parents cook, and later I began watching cooking shows on TV. I watched Graham Kerr three times a day. One Christmas, when I was four, I received a toy kitchen with plastic cutlery and utensils and everything in it. To act like I had my own show, I asked Dad to videotape me in my new kitchen while I made a vegetable pot pie. My father sent the tape to Graham Kerr, the Galloping Gourmet, because he was my favorite chef and still is to this day. Graham Kerr sent back an autographed letter [that read], "Justin, you do very well. But when you're four, you don't chop and talk at the same time like the chefs on TV, you do only one thing." So Graham Kerr said, "Remember Justin, while you're chopping, make sure you keep talking. Chopping and talking. Do that, and in seven years I'll move over, and you can take my place [as a TV chef]."

When we received that letter, my dad contacted the *Beaver County Time*s in Pennsylvania. Reporters came over and I made lunch for them. After the lunch, the reporters wrote a full-page article on me for the *Times*. My dad videotaped that event and sent a copy of the article with a compilation video-tape to David Letterman. Within two days, we heard that David Letterman wanted me on his show. Since then, I've had more than two hundred TV appearances, including being a regular guest on the *Mike and Maty Show*, a network talk show.

K&G: What changes have you seen in your cooking abilities from when you started until today?

The recipe I am most known for is my mini-cheesecake, which I developed when I was five. Since then, I have seen a lot of changes in my style and ability. In fact, I'm creating something similar to a chicken crescent roll-up, and I also have a signature dish called Mushroom Mountain. The biggest difference in my style is that I'm moving toward cooking more entrées.

K&G: Do you go to cooking classes or cooking school?

During the summer, I attend Johnson and Wales University, where I learn new cooking techniques. My favorite instructor there, Rick Tarantino, has taught me the right ways to do things. If I don't do something properly, like holding the utensils, he takes the time to show me the proper way. It's amazing how involved it gets, even with whisking. If you just grab the whisk and start doing it, your wrist will get tired. Proper technique is essential. Some of the lessons I take are knife skills, sautéing skills, and flambéing skills. I enjoy the one-on-one cooking lessons.

K&G: Are you involved in other organizations, such as charities?

I'm involved with the Kids With a Cause program and some other charitable organizations like the March of Dimes, the American Heart Association, and the Audrey Hepburn Children's Fund. I've also been the chef host for two Academy Awards dinners benefiting kids in Los Angeles.

Currently I'm the spokesperson for a new program called "Mix It with Milk," sponsored by the Dairy Council. I get to do demonstrations with second graders and teach them how to create different concoctions [with milk]. I try to get kids very involved in cooking. I know they can do it, too. I like to teach and inspire other kids to cook.

K&G: What has been the largest event so far in your career?

The biggest event I've had the opportunity to attend is either the *David Letterman Show* or the ACF [American Culinary Federation] convention. The ACF convention is a big conference and demonstration event for all the chefs around the world to show off their recipes. I was the first-ever ambassador to the American Culinary Federation Chef and Child Foundation [ACFCCF].

K&G: How do you create new recipes?

I just go into the kitchen, grab some different ingredients, and see what it turns out like. I set aside time a couple of times a week to experiment with new recipes.

K&G: What has been the most fun you have had throughout this experience?

The most fun I've experienced by doing this is being on TV as many times as I have and meeting great people like Michael J. Fox and David Copperfield. It's also been fun to create my cookbooks, *Cooking with Justin* and *Break an Egg*. I developed *Cooking with Justin* when I was seven. I compiled all my favorite recipes and also included knock-knock jokes for kids. I tried to keep it fun. It has some simple recipes with fun names that are easy for kids to cook. *Break an Egg* is coming out soon.

K&G: How can other kids become chefs?

Just go for it! It's a lot of fun once you get into it. Be careful taking stuff in and out of the oven. Start out with a simple recipe at home with your family. Try to have as much adult supervision as you can in the kitchen. You can never have too much of that. Be careful and have fun.

K&G: What is your vision for the future?

One of my main goals is to own a restaurant. Another dream I have is to have my own cooking show. I'd have my own show now, but there is a liability issue because of my age. A lot of television networks want me to do a show, but they are afraid of getting sued because kids might watch me and then hurt themselves by imitating what I do in the kitchen. I use extreme care in the kitchen and try to teach safety to other kids. The networks thought about having an adult chop all the ingredients, but that doesn't show my talents. As soon as we figure out a way to do it, I'll have my own show. It'll be cool if it happens before I'm eighteen.

Wrap-Up

What can you do to invest in yourself? Take a class, ask for help, find a mentor, or just believe in the possibilities. You have many choices to make to attain your dream. Justin has always known that he loves to cook and that it's what he wants to do with his life. As a kid, he made a choice to make his dream of being a chef come true. He didn't wait until he became an adult. He found mentors, took classes, and explored many different avenues of his craft, such as writing books and working with charities. Exploring your passion can be just one way of investing in yourself.

Contact Information

To reach Justin, go to http://www.chefjustin.com/, or contact him in care of his agent:

Justin Miller
Agent: Bonnie Shumofsky
Abrams Artists Agency
275 7th Avenue
New York, New York 10001
(646) 486-4601, ext. 357
Bonnie.Shumofsky@abramsart.com

CHAPTER 7

Confidence

Confidence is the feeling that tells you to trust in your abilities and be proud of who you are, *no matter what*. The most important part of this statement is "no matter what." Be proud of who you are no matter what choices you make, how things turn out, or what you wish you could have done differently. Be proud of who you are despite any internal feelings you might have about how you look or how you're different. Be confident; no matter what package you come in, you are a gift! Having confidence doesn't mean that you know or need to know everything. It simply means that you have enough self-belief to give new things a try.

Being confident about yourself and your idea sells that idea and shows that you are serious about what you are doing. It can also play a key role in the success of your dream. When you communicate with others, does your confidence show? Here are a few characteristics that can help you find out:

- **Body Language:** What does your body language tell people around you?
  Tip: To exude confidence, stand or sit up straight, look people in the eye, and remember to connect with your inner strength.

- **Voice:** How are you communicating your ideas?
  Tip: Speak up, speak clearly, stay focused, and show strength in your voice. This doesn't mean yelling, but make sure you are heard and understood.

● **Enthusiasm:** What is your excitement level?

Tip: Show excitement about your idea. You know it's a great idea; let others know it, too!

● **Sincerity:** Are you being true and honest?

Tip: Be honest and genuine. People shy away from those who lie or are not genuine. Sincerity is a quality that others can feel, so be honest in all situations.

● **Uniqueness:** Are you being yourself or who others want you to be?

Tip: Stay true to yourself and your own ideas. You don't have to change to please others. Be willing to show others what makes you and your idea one of a kind.

● **Pride:** Are you proud of your ideas or embarrassed and shy about them?

Tip: Be proud of your creativity and abilities. Show that you have pride in your ideas.

● **Mistakes:** How do you handle making mistakes or bad choices?

Tip: Everyone makes mistakes and bad choices once in a while. Move past them by realizing that you aren't going to be perfect all the time and that you can use your mistakes to learn how to make better choices. Accept your mistakes, do the best you can, and be proud of your efforts.

Finding your confidence can be a work in progress. Keep building on it with each new step you take. If you feel your confidence needs some improvement, here are two techniques that you can try:

Visualization: Visualize the things you wish to accomplish and see yourself achieving success. Here's how: Think of an area where you would like some added confidence. Imagine a situation where having this confidence will come into play. Now imagine behaving with confidence in this situation. What would you say and what would you do? How is your behavior different? Keep imagining this success. Then the next time you are faced with a situation, remember what you did differently and how you handled this situation in your visualization. Know that you do have confidence. You can use visualization with any goal you would like to accomplish. Get into the habit of visualizing your victories every day. Never allow yourself to visualize failing. If any negativity creeps into your thoughts, immediately change it to something positive. Your actions will follow your thoughts. If you visualize success, you move toward success. If you visualize failure, you move toward failure.

✎ Choose success and write down a goal you would like to visualize yourself accomplishing.

Positive Self-Talk: Self-talk is the practice of talking to yourself in your head. Some people call such talk "tapes" because they can be thoughts or opinions that you've heard and recorded and then repeated over and over to yourself. For example, imagine that you are trying a new sport and someone you are playing with makes fun of you and tells you that you aren't cut out for sports. What you do with that opinion will help determine your own self-talk. You might believe that what that person told you is true, record the thought, and begin telling yourself that you aren't good at playing sports. This is an example of negative self-talk and one of the factors that will determine how your beliefs about yourself are formed. Can you imagine never trying sports again because one person told you weren't very good? Positive self-talk would allow you to disregard the negative comment and instead tell yourself you can do anything you dream of. Just remember to stay focused on your positive strengths and you will remain confident when trying sports or other new things.

Your own self-talk and how you allow other people's words affect you is a good indicator of how confident you are. Sometimes your self-talk is unconscious, which means that you often are not even aware of what you say to yourself. When these unconscious thoughts are negative, they can be very damaging to your self-esteem. To avoid negativity, start observing the things you say to yourself and get into the habit of surrounding yourself with positive self-talk and affirmations. Focus on the positive aspects of who you are and what you are capable of doing; remember your unique qualities and feel confident about them.

Sometimes affirmations—or statements designed to bring about positive change in oneself or one's environment—start with "I am," but try the trick of saying "I am" at the end. This adds strength to your words. Here are a variety of affirmations to get you started. You can say them out loud or in your head or write them in a journal: *Confident, I am. Strong, I am. Successful, I am. Amazing, I am. Proud, I am, of myself and my choices. Beautiful, I am. Special, I am. An amazing gift, I am!*

Some other ways to stay positive and confident with your self-talk is to think of what you love about yourself and remind yourself of these qualities on a regular basis: *I love how creative I can be. I love my talents. I love my uniqueness. I love my sense of humor. I love how well I communicate. I love how quickly I can solve problems. I love being a risk taker. I believe in me. Anything is possible. I can do this. I can achieve anything I dream is possible. If someone says something negative about me, I will disregard that thought.*

✎ These are just a few examples to get you started. So that they are always on hand when you need them, take this time to write down affirmations and positive self-talk that fit you and your specific goals and dreams.

Are you feeling confident about yourself and your idea? Imagine this scenario and think about what you would do: Someone important to you makes a suggestion to "improve" an idea that you have, but you feel that the idea changes your vision. What do you do? Do you take the suggestion and make changes to your idea to avoid any conflict between the two of you? Do you stand by your original idea and not change it? Or do you compromise some-where in the middle? If you want to stick to your idea, what could you say to the person who suggested improvements that thanks him or her for the input but makes it clear that you are confident in your choice of leaving the idea as it is? ✍ Take some time now to write down some possible statements that could be used for each scenario. Include some general ways of how you can boost your confidence. If you need some inspiration, read our interview with Rachael Scdoris, whom we met in her hometown of Bend, Oregon.

LET'S DO IT!

Rachael Scdoris
age 17
Bend, oregon

professional sled
Dog Racer

"Keep at it, even when it gets hard. Once you get past the hard points, it's all downhill from there!"

Rachael's interview was unique in that we hung out with Rachael and her dad, Jerry, for a day and a half. We spent that time watching and participating in Rachael's training. It was exciting to see what Rachael goes through to train as a professional sled dog racer. On Saturday she was up by 7:00 AM to get the dogs ready while Jerry prepared the roads. Watching Rachael maneuver through her environment was amazing. She trained on a three-mile winding dirt road on a special sled with tires instead of her typical snow sled, since it hadn't snowed yet. She and her team of dogs maneuvered every corner, bump, and ditch with ease and grace. As we watched Rachael train, it was hard to believe that she is not a sighted person. She is bold, confident, and exact in her movements. During Rachael's interview, she shared her belief that obstacles are merely bumps in the road, and if she's going fast enough, she doesn't even feel them.

Meet Rachael

If you try to tell Rachael that she can't do something, she will confidently say, "Just watch me." Rachael's inner strength and confidence have propelled her to be a top professional competitor in sled dog racing. If everything works out just right, Rachael will overcome the odds to participate in her first Iditarod race, a sled dog race held in Alaska every March that covers 1,150 miles in ten to seventeen days.

K&G: How did you become a professional sled dog racer?

I started because of my dad. He's had dogs since the 1970s, so I was sort of born into it. He always used to take me out on sledding runs with him. [When I was little] I'd beg him to let me take the team out. Finally when I was about eight or nine, he let me take two dogs out on a one-mile loop. I started sled dog racing at age eleven, but I've had the dogs my whole life. I'm a professional sled dog racer and the youngest person to ever complete a 500-mile race. My first big competition was a 500-mile Wyoming race. The race was so long that I started when I was fifteen and finished when I was sixteen!

K&G: Besides being one of the youngest professional sled dog racers, what else is unique about your racing career?

What makes my story especially unique is that I have a vision disorder called Congenital Achromatopsia. That means I can't see fine detail and I can't really tell colors apart. I'm not totally color-blind. I can see colors, but a lot of them just look the same. I can't really see things far away. In order to read, I have to hold whatever I'm reading about three inches from my eyes. Legally, I'm considered to be blind.

K&G: What is it like to be a professional sled dog racer?

To drive the sled, I often go by how the sled feels. People expect me to have great hearing, but, honestly, my hearing is just like everyone else's. Believe it or not, I'm a visual learner. I don't think this is a disadvantage for me. I say it's only a disadvantage if I let it be a disadvantage, like anything else.

Right now, I attend one or two big competitions a year and go to little ones around Oregon just for fun, to watch mostly. The two major competitions I've been in, and that I'm going to compete in again this year, are the Atta Boy 300 here in Oregon and the 500-miler in Wyoming. I might compete in a 200-miler in Montana as well.

The Atta Boy 300 lasts seven days, including the ceremonial start and vet check. The Wyoming race takes twelve days, including the ceremonial start and vet check. The Montana race, which I may or may not run, is straight through. It generally lasts one to three days, depending on how your team runs.

We work with about ninety dogs and we run different numbers of dogs in different competitions. Some competitions run only two dogs and some run an unlimited number. I generally run eight to twelve dogs in a competition. The length of the races can be anywhere from four to one hundred miles in one day.

A typical day for me in the Atta Boy 300 race starts when I'm woken up at six in the morning by one of my handlers, who are there to take care of the dogs for me. Then we drive to the staging area, where we prepare to race. We harness the dogs, take care of their feed if needed, pack my sled with all the mandatory gear, and then I race for anywhere from two to five hours, depending on how long the trail is that day. When I'm finished with that leg of the race, the handlers and I get water for the dogs, put the dogs away, put all the equipment away, and then usually just drive straight to the banquet that's held that night. My handlers take care of the dogs while I eat. After that, we go to our host family's house, and if I'm not too tired, I'll help my handlers with the dogs a little bit and then go to bed.

Depending on the race, there are a varying number of competing teams. In the Atta Boy this January, there will be forty teams. In Wyoming there will probably be twenty. Some races have limits on how many teams can compete, but in others any number of teams can race.

K&G: Who has helped you?

The people who have played the biggest role in my success are both my parents, my friends, the people who work with my dad at the sled dog tour company, my coaches, and Frank Teasley, who puts on the race in Wyoming every year. He was the first person who invited me to race. I also have to thank Dan MacEachen, who was my first snow machine guide [a visual interpreter who uses a walkie-talkie to warn dogsledders about obstacles on the trail, such as low hanging branches or broken ice].

K&G: At what age can someone race in competitions?

The competitions are full of people of all ages. I think in order to participate in the World Cup or to race a certain amount of miles, you have to be over sixteen years old because it would be dangerous to allow a ten- or eleven-year-old to race and possibly get hurt. But there are all kinds of recreational races for younger kids, who are called Peewees, where just one dog pulls the sled and the race is only 100 yards. There's also the novice competition, which has a four-dog limit and usually runs one to four miles. Then there are four-dog class, six-dog class, and eight-dog class races. A lot of kids like to participate in those.

K&G: Are there a lot of women in professional dog sled racing?

There aren't a lot of women in this field. Although there are more now than there ever have been before, the sport is still dominated by men. The women who compete do really well, though.

K&G: What is involved with being a professional dog sled racer?

Doing this takes some hard work, organization—which I don't have, but fortunately my handlers do—and good dogs. You also have to be a pretty good athlete to be able to run up the hills and control the sled on the way down. You have to be able to react to anything that might be thrown at you.

To train for the races, I have to get a lot of miles on my dogs. In the fall, we're running the dogs in three-mile laps. As soon as it rains, we'll start taking them on 17-mile runs and then work up to 30 miles. Once it snows in the mountains, we'll go up there and get some real sledding miles on the dogs. As for myself, I'm doing weight training and cross-country running. As soon as that's over, my coach has agreed to start hill training.

There are a lot of people involved in my sled dog racing. I have sponsors, my parents, my entire family, the handlers— usually two per race—people who work with my dad doing the commercial sled dog tours, volunteers, and friends.

K&G: What has been your biggest obstacle?

My biggest obstacle is people saying I couldn't do it. There are people concerned about my safety and then there are other people not wanting to accept that a blind person can do well against them. That's been my biggest obstacle—just people who don't know me and what I'm capable of. As far as I'm concerned, allowing my vision to limit me would just be silly.

K&G: What has been the most fun you have had throughout this experience?

I think the thing I like most about sled dog racing are the dogs. They're so sweet! The running part is a delightful bonus. I'm just out there playing with my dogs!

K&G: Who inspires you?

The most inspirational people in my life are my parents and Marla Runyon, a runner who also has vision difficulties. She has a different disorder than I do, but her vision is similar and she went to the Olympics a couple of years ago. George Attla, who is one of the legends of our sport, is also an inspiration to me. He had tuberculosis when he was a kid and he's also had one of his knees fused. But he has still won many races and world championships. He's an inspiration to many people. My long-time hero is Libby Riddles, who was the first woman to win the Iditarod.

K&G: What do your friends think of you as a professional sled dog racer?

Most of the kids at my school don't know I'm a sled dog racer, but the ones who do know think it's very cool. I don't get teased about my sight as much as I did when I was little. I don't notice that kind of teasing nearly as much as I notice being teased about being a female! When that happens, I challenge the person who's teasing me to a race around the track or to a wrestling match.

K&G: How can other kids become professional sled dog racers?

I'd tell other kids who were thinking of becoming a sled dog racer, "Good for you!" It's a lot of work but it's a lot more fun. Start locally with two- or three-mile races with two or three dogs, then work your way up. If you still like it, try being a dog handler for a racer if you can. I've learned a lot by handling dogs for my dad. Handling dogs will teach you a lot about everything that goes on in a race. You mostly learn to be a sled dog racer through trial and error. I have a dad who's very experienced, so he was able to help me avoid a lot of errors, but that's mostly how you learn stuff—by making mistakes and saying, "I won't do that again!" Keep at it even when it gets hard. Once you get past the hard points, it's all downhill from there.

K&G: What is your vision for the future?
I want to keep on sled dog racing until I get tired of it, which will be quite a while.

My dreams right now are to win the Iditarod during my rookie year. It's a long shot, but a good dream. And to be world champion eventually, and go to the Olympics as a runner.

As far as running goes, I went to the Olympic Trials with the United States Association of Blind Athletes to run in an exhibition 400-meter race. I'm not a 400-meter runner, but I still got third place, so I'm hoping to run in the 1,500-, the 5,000-, or the 10,000-meter races.

My goals this year in track and field are to break 22 [minutes] in the 5,000-meter race, hopefully be in the low 520s [seconds] in the 1,500, and break 11 [minutes] in the 3,000. I also want to go to the Paralympics in Athens. The Paralympics are the Olympics for people who have some sort of physical limitation but who are truly good athletes; they are just short of making the Olympics. Hopefully I'll make that team if I don't make the Olympics.

Right now, I'm in pretty good World Cup standings for professional sled dog racing. I expect to be in at least the top twenty with the two races I'll run this year. As far as winning the world championship, being World Cup champion, or winning the Iditarod, it's all going to take a lot of work.

Wrap-Up

Confidence can be gained through life experiences or it can be learned. Rachael is confident in her abilities, her beliefs, and her possibilities. She uses her inner strengths and confidence to help her accomplish her goals. Take a look at yourself. Are you confident? Do you use your confidence to help you achieve your dreams? If not, use your passion and inspiration along with the guidance you've found in this book to help you develop your confidence. You will be amazed at what you can accomplish once you become confident in yourself and your abilities!

Contact Information
To reach Rachael, go to http://www.sleddogrides.com/.

Inspire

Inspire and be inspired. Whether you are selling a product, inventing a toy, or starting a volunteer group—whatever the idea—there will be a time when you have to get your idea out there and present it to others. The key to getting others excited about your idea is to show them your excitement and passion about it. Excitement and enthusiasm are powerful forces. Your ideas sell when others feel your energy and want to be a part of it.

Imagine for a moment that someone is trying to sell you a product, but when she pitches the product she speaks in a monotone voice and seems uninterested in what she is doing. You might even find it hard to pay attention to what she is saying. Would you want to buy the product? Probably not. What do you think is missing?

What convinces people that something has value or is beneficial is the enthusiasm and passion the promoter has for it. When you're communicating your idea to people, remember: This is your vision you are talking about. Let others see it through your eyes. Show your enthusiasm, excitement, and energy! Open your heart and reveal why your product or idea is important to you and why it should be important to them. When you do, people will more likely want to be a part of it.

There are many ways to stay inspired. Bring daily inspiration to your project by using some of the following ideas:

● Find activities that refuel your creativity. Do something creative through writing, painting, or something else you enjoy. Or change your perspective by exploring nature while on a hike or walking on the beach. An activity that refuels you should be incorporated into your daily schedule.

● Build a support group. Find people you can brainstorm or create with. Spend time with people who support your idea and encourage you in positive ways. Create synergy around your idea; the more support and encouragement you feel, the more inspired and creative you will be with your idea. Having a support circle is essential. Nobody does it alone.

● Find examples of inspiration in your field. Read about others who have gone before you. Broaden your perspective of what is possible by understanding what has already been done. Allow the experiences of those who have gone before you to be your platform for success.

● Find mentors or other people you can rely on for sound, positive advice. They could be your parents or a teacher, someone from your church or community center, or a local businessperson. Mentors can provide guidance by sharing their own life experiences. Be willing to listen and make them a part of your circle.

Remember to stay enthusiastic about your idea. Convey your passion whether you are selling your product or idea or simply sharing your idea with others. Show people why they should love your idea as much as you do. When inspiration motivates your ideas, creativity flows more easily, solutions pop up unexpectedly, your confidence builds, and others become inspired to search for what they feel passionate about. If you don't feel inspired or passionate about your idea, you might consider finding an idea for which you do.

✍ Why are you passionate about your idea? Pretend that you need someone's help and you are sharing your idea to inspire him to get involved. What can you do or say to show him your passion? Take a minute to write down some ideas.

✍ What are some fun ways you can come up with to stay connected to your inspiration? Use some of the ideas mentioned in this chapter as a model, if you'd like, then jot down your own ideas in your chapter. If you need help getting started, check out the following interview with Ryan Patterson, the inventor of the American Sign Language Translator.

LET'S DO IT!

Ryan Patterson

Age 18
Grand Junction,
Colorado

Inventor of the
American Sign
Language (ASL)
Translator

"Don't worry about what other [kids] think about you."

We met Ryan at his home in Grand Junction, Colorado, where we interviewed him in his office/lab. Three-ring binders were lined up on the shelves along one wall of the room; medals that Ryan had won at various science fairs decorated a corner of the room; and computers and equipment filled the rest of the space. During the interview, Ryan gave us a demonstration of the American Sign Language (ASL) Translator, a glove that converts the ASL alphabet—hand signs for each letter of the American alphabet—to written text on a portable display. It was amazing to see how his mind had taken an idea and turned it into a successful tool. It felt, in some small way, like we were in Thomas Edison's lab, surrounded by amazing ideas and inventions just waiting to be brought to life.

Ryan truly exhibits greatness, not solely because of his invention and what it means to the world, but because of his ability to envision his idea as a successful creation.

Meet Ryan

Ryan's passion for electronics and his desire to help others led him to create an invention that has won him top honors in multiple competitions. One of these competitions was Intel's 2002 Science Talent Search, often referred to as "the junior Nobel prize," where Ryan won a $100,000 scholarship. His passion, which started at an early age, continues to grow and inspire many who cross his path.

K&G: How did your passion for electronics begin?

When I was as young as I can remember, I'd drag around an extension cord instead of a blanket. I've just always been interested in electronics. When I was young I loved learning about electronics. I'd take things apart and put them back together. Eventually, my grandpa and I, and then my dad and I, made simple robots that moved around. I learned about the motors that control machines like robots. As I got older, I did more things with electronics. In third grade I started working with a mentor who had a lot to teach me. That's how I got to where I am. I went to my mentor's house all day every Saturday and he'd teach me all about electronics.

In fifth and sixth grades, I competed in robotic competitions. In one competition, my mentor was the oldest person participating and I was the youngest. As a team, we did very well and won three gold medals and one bronze medal.

K&G: How did your passion for electronics turn into inventing?

I competed in science fairs for years before I designed the ASL translator. I did a new project every year. One year I built a device that detected electromagnetic fields. The next year, I worked with electronic neuronetworks, which are basically walking robots. After that, I did research on artificial intelligence and created a mazebot, which is a robot that can find its way through a maze. A couple of years later, I designed a robot that could search buildings in a crisis situation. The robot was very small and had a video camera, sonar, and a microphone on it. It could see in the dark and move at high speeds, so it could search a building very quickly. You could control it from a computer from a mile away. I won Best in Engineering, as well as a number of other awards, for that invention that year at the Intel Science Fair. That was my first big year. The next year, at the International Science Fair, I presented the ASL glove and won the grand prize. After that, I competed in the Siemens Westinghouse Competition in Math, Science, & Technology, as well as other big competitions.

To be this successful, I've just worked really hard at it over the years and have been very persistent in this one area of electronics. I have no problem sitting at a workbench all day every Saturday, learning how to read schematics and that type of thing. I was lucky to get to work with a mentor—that was a huge part of my success. My mentor made the biggest difference to the course of my life and what I wanted to do with it.

Since winning the Intel Science Talent Search for the ASL Translator, my life has been crazy. I've received a lot of recognition. It's been fun. Even though I spent hundreds of hours developing my invention, it was definitely worth [all of] the rewards [it has] brought. For years, I spent all my time on projects and didn't receive much recognition, so this has been a lot of fun. It's been an honor to get to do so many things.

K&G: What inspires you to invent?

My inspiration comes during the research and development of an idea, when I'm learning about new things. I really enjoy doing the research and learning more about electronics. I really get into it. Once I start a project, I can easily stay up all night working on it, even sitting at the computer for hours without moving, writing code, and designing circuit boards. I guess it's just something I have such an interest in that it's easy to do.

K&G: What inspired you to invent the ASL Translator?
When I was sixteen, I was looking for a project to do for a science fair. I saw a group of people using sign language in a restaurant. They had an interpreter for when they needed to communicate with people who didn't know sign language. I thought that it would be more convenient if they had an electronic interpreter. It would help make them more independent because they wouldn't have to rely on another person to translate for them. It sounded like a fun project to me. If I'm going to spend nine months or so working on a project, I want it to be something I'll have fun with.

K&G: What were the steps you took to invent the ASL Translator?
First I did some research on ASL to prove that it would be a worthwhile project to do. After that, I needed to choose which microcontroller to use as a device to transmit data, learn the microcontroller's language, and develop circuit boards. I designed the circuit boards on the computer and then e-mailed the design to a company that made them for me. They sent me back the boards and I soldered all the components on. I did testing and then spent about a month on programming and building the portable display. It was a real push to do all that within a month, because that much work usually takes about three to four months.

Most days, I worked on the project about three hours. I had three high school classes, two college classes, and work; then I'd come home and do my homework, and work on the ASL translator. I didn't sleep much during that month! I also taught myself the ASL alphabet during this time.

79

I had the first prototype of the translator running in about six months [which was used for testing]. Over the next two months, I worked really hard and got the portable translator working. I slowly made improvements over the summer, but most of the work was done in those first eight months.

To use the glove, a person must first train the computer to his or her method of signing; it's kind of like voice recognition. Through a circuit board [the glove interprets the ASL alphabet, letter by letter] by reading the data from ten sensors on the glove that detect finger and wrist movements. [When someone wearing the glove signs a letter in the ASL alphabet, an *A* for example, the sensors collect data on the hand's positions and then send this data to a tiny microcontroller or minicomputer in the glove. The computer then sends a wireless signal to a receiver, which translates the data and displays the letter *A*.]

To use it, you sign a letter and pause. Then the device displays the letter on the screen. It could be used for training young students, but I think the main application is just as a translator.

K&G: What do your friends think of your interest in electronics?

Friends don't categorize me as a science nerd; they treat me just like I'm one of them. [In fact] my friends think that what I do is really cool, especially since I drive a great car that I was able to buy with award money I've gotten from the science. In the last few months of my senior year, I've had media groups following me around school, and other students would try to get in front of the camera to get some media exposure [too].

K&G: What has been the most fun you have had throughout this experience?

The most fun I've been able to have so far is when I went to Sweden for the Nobel Prize ceremonies. I really enjoyed that. That was the best experience I've ever had. I've gotten to meet lots of people at the science conferences I've attended. At every competition, there are two or three people I meet whom I stay in touch with afterwards. After years of competing, that adds up. I've made more friends across the nation than I probably have here in Grand Junction.

K&G: What has been the least fun you have had throughout this experience?

The scariest moments for me were my first few times presenting in front of a big group. I was a little bit nervous. It was also scary the first few times I traveled by myself. During my freshman year, I went to New Orleans by myself to work for eight weeks. I was a little bit nervous before leaving for the trip. The thing I like least about what I do is documenting my processes. I keep a journal and write maybe a page every other day about what I'm doing with my current project and then use that information to write big reports or presentations. I like the development, not the paperwork. The only challenge for me is the publicity I've received. It is extremely time consuming. I probably spend eight to ten hours a week with the media [being interviewed].

K&G: How can other kids become inventors?

It depends on the field. If you are interested in electronics, I'd go to Radio Shack. They have a lot of books to introduce you to electronics. Teach yourself as much as you can. I read all the books that I could get my parents to buy for me when I was little. Show your parents that you are serious and that it isn't something that you have an interest in for only a month. My mentor said that's what was really different about me—that I was born with a passion in one area. He saw right away that I had always been that way and I always would be. That's why he worked with me.

Get involved in science competitions. You'll meet kids who have been interested in their fields for most of their lives. They will go far because they are persistent. Stick with it and you'll go far, too. When I was little, I did not have resources, but I just kept playing with electronics. If I met people who knew anything about electronics, I'd ask them a million questions. I was always asking my teachers questions even though I knew they couldn't answer them. I think that's what pushed one of them to find me a mentor. Show that you have a huge interest. I think you'll probably end up finding some sort of a resource to help you out.

Don't worry about what the other students think about you, especially in middle school. I think some kids who have an interest in science lose that interest in middle school and maybe a little bit in high school because of pressure from their peers. I didn't have good friends in middle school. Everybody teased me and made things really hard because of my interest in science. In high school, students were a lot more respectful. Instead of being a nerdy thing, a lot of people thought it was cool. If you've got an interest in something, then you're ahead of the kids who don't know what they want to do. Keep that in mind if they're giving you trouble. Just think, in the future, you'll be a big step ahead of them if you pursue what you're interested in as early as you can.

K&G: What is your vision for the future?

I'm going to college in a few days, and then I don't know what will happen from there. I'll be studying electrical and computer engineering. I'm looking forward to learning more. My mentor taught me all that he could, and I've been teaching myself what I can, mainly about programming and computers. I'm looking forward to being able to continue my learning over the next few years.

I don't really know what's going to happen next. I've applied for a patent on the ASL translator, but it could take up to two years to find out what happens. I definitely want to do something with the glove. I would like to see it on the market because it could help a lot of people. I'll push to get it there.

In the future, I don't want to have to spend all my time owning and running a business. I wouldn't be happy doing that. Even if I were making a lot of money, that's not my interest. I'd rather be a developer—an engineer working in a lab to develop this type of device [like the ASL Translator].

Wrap-Up

Ryan finds inspiration in his passion for electronics. There are some things he would rather not do, like documenting his processes, but Ryan knows that they are all part of his dream. Ryan uses his passion as motivation to get the best results. A very tangible result is the more than $400,000 in college scholarships he's received.

What inspires you? Look at what you are passionate about to find inspiration and motivation. If you find yourself running out of energy, change your routine to include advice you have gotten in this chapter. Use the inspiration you feel to propel you to the next level of your dream. Be inspired by what you are capable of accomplishing!

Contact Information

To reach Ryan, e-mail him at ryan@planetgiggle.com.

section 4

Magic

Magic

The magic we are talking about is not the rabbit-out-of-a-hat kind, but it's not too far off. You see, in that magic trick, the rabbit seems to appear from nowhere. There's really no reasonable explanation of how it works, so how does it happen?

If you've studied magic before, you can probably guess, but for the rest of us non-magic folk, we have no clue. As much as we would like to try to figure it out, we accept that there are unknown steps in magic that must take place in order for the impossible to happen.

The same is true with dreams. In order for them to happen, you have to know or accept that unknown or unforeseen occurrences will take place. That is the magic of following a dream. You may not know how it will work, but you must know that it can.

In this section, explore the magic of your dream by learning to trust and listen to your inner guidance.

CHAPTER 9

Truѕt

Many times, trust is defined as having confidence and faith in someone or something outside of ourselves. But what would you think if you were told that trust is something that should be placed in yourself instead of in others?

The essential truth behind trust is placing faith and confidence in yourself, your own choices, and your ability to handle anything that comes your way. You can't control the actions of others and you can't completely control the outcome of a situation, so you must trust yourself to handle whatever comes along. The good news is that clues exist all around you to guide you in the right direction. Be observant. Here are some of the signs to look for:

- **Your gut feeling.** Deep down, how do you feel about the person or situation? Do you feel uneasy, uncomfortable, or that something is not quite right? Maybe you feel excited, happy, and like everything is OK. Trust that first gut feeling to guide you.

- **Observation.** Pay attention to how events unfold. Take note of recurring situations. Past behavior can help you predict future behavior. For example, if someone has lied to you in the past, even though he has told you that he would never do it again, would you want to place your faith in that person's promise to help with something important for your project? Probably not. When you are looking for people to work with, make sure that you trust their behaviors. Their actions are good indicators

87

and can help you predict what to expect from them. Trust people's actions over their words.

● **Body language.** Notice what isn't being said by watching people's nonverbal communication. If you are speaking to someone, does she make eye contact with you? Does she face you or turn away? Does she seem confident or fidgety? If people are fidgety and don't make a lot of eye contact, their body language indicates that they are uncomfortable, and it may mean that they aren't being totally honest with you. Pay attention to people's actions and learn to trust what you see.

Ultimately, trust comes down to you and the choices you make for yourself. Trust your own inner strength and inner guidance to lead you. Follow your passion and inspiration. Sometimes you may have to disregard what others tell you. Rather than placing your trust in the outcome of a situation, trust yourself to handle any situation that comes along.

So what does all this have to do with your dream? At each new step, new and unforeseen opportunities and situations will arise. It's like going through a maze. There is no way to see around each corner to know what new choices you will have, so trust is incredibly important. People may question your ideas, your intentions, even your ability to succeed. People may lie to you or things may not turn out exactly the way you had expected. You can't predict how everything is going to take place; you just have to trust that even if you can't see all the "hows" to making it work, things will fall into place as you move along. Put your trust in a bigger picture, where everything that happens makes sense and serves a purpose. Understand that there are unseen forces—the magic we discussed—that align with you and help you when you follow your dream. As you follow a dream, you don't have to know how it will happen; you just have to know that it can.

✍ What are some issues of trust that have come up in your life or in your project? Did this chapter give you any ideas on how you can exercise trust in yourself? Use your chapter to note thoughts you might have. How would you like to learn to trust yourself more as you work toward accomplishing your dream?

The following interview with Elise and Evan Macmillan, CEOs of the Chocolate Farm, shows you just how far trusting yourself can take you.

LET'S DO IT!

Elise and Evan Macmillan
Ages 13 and 16
Denver, Colorado

CEOs of the Chocolate Farm

"Having faith in yourself and your dream and following through on an idea can lead to so much success."

We met Elise and Evan at their offices in Denver, Colorado, where we were greeted with the heavenly aroma of chocolate. We were quite impressed when we walked into their offices, which included a reception/waiting area, an area for preparing orders, an area for inventory, and a large conference room with an office. Seeing two kids operate in such a professional environment seemed out of place at first, but when the interview started, we understood that Evan and Elise are quite comfortable in their space and in their business. Make no mistake: the Chocolate Farm is a legitimate, successful business with kids as the Chief Executive

Officers (CEOs). Elise and Evan have a great sibling connection that was evident throughout their interview as well as in the structure and operation of their business. After the interview we toured the kitchen where all the wonderful chocolate treats are made. And, yes, we got some chocolate for the road, and it was delicious.

Meet Elise and Evan

Elise and Evan used their love for making chocolate to create an extraordinary hobby. Before they knew it, that hobby took off and turned into a very successful business. In 2001 the Chocolate Farm was rated the top youth food business in the United States. Elise and Evan's inspiring story continues to receive national attention, and it proves that dreams really can come true at any age.

K&G: How did you start your own Internet chocolate company?

Elise: It all started about three years ago when Evan encouraged us to sell our first chocolates at a Youth Holiday Marketplace sponsored by the Young Americans Bank [YAB].

Evan: The YAB is a local bank here in Denver. It's really unique in the fact that everybody who opens an account has to be under the age of twenty-two, so it provides a unique opportunity for kids and teens. They can open an account, gain experience with money, learn how to write checks, and use an ATM card. YAB also teaches classes in entrepreneurship. I was lucky enough to be a youth advisory board member for the bank, which gave me a lot of experience with the management team of the bank.

Every year YAB puts on a Youth Workplace and Workshop where kids can sell their wares and services to the general public. It is heavily promoted in the community. In the process of working with the bank to get people to come out, I told Elise that we needed to do something because it would be a really great opportunity to try our hand at a business. The night before the workshop, the Chocolate

Farm was born. We had no big intentions but the first day went really well. We sold a few hundred dollars' worth of chocolate, and it has been growing ever since.

Elise: We decided to sell chocolate at the Youth Holiday Market-place because we love chocolate and our grandma taught us how to make it when we were really young. We thought that most people love chocolate, and what would be more fun to do than make chocolate? We really wanted a theme for our chocolate instead of just Elise and Evan's chocolates. Since our grand-parents grew up on a farm and we love animals, we decided on a farm theme. We thought it was just going to be a one-day thing, but a lot of people really loved it and kept ordering chocolate. So we kept going. At first it was just a hobby, but it turned into a business. We were excited. We thought we could use the busi-ness to make some money and have some fun doing it.

K&G: How did a one-day sale turn into a business?
Evan: Our biggest step to creating a business was the develop-ment of a Web site. It became a really great tool for us to help promote the business. When you're small, you can't always go out and have your own retail location. The Web made it really easy to put out our catalogue so people would have the oppor-tunity to buy things and see who we were. It became a really important and valuable tool for our company. After that day at the Holiday Marketplace, we were lucky enough to be fea-tured in the *Denver Post* newspaper. That same day, *People* magazine called, and that led to a whole string of L.A. and New York talk shows. One thing led to another, and although we weren't even thinking about our business like it was a big thing, each of the interviews continued to provide us with more business and put our name out there.

We were so lucky to be carried on by one thing after another. By taking that risk and taking the first—and hardest—step to put ourselves out there, we found that everything else works itself out. We are fortunate it has worked out so well.

Elise: In the beginning our sales were all word of mouth. People who were at the marketplace told their friends, and we received more orders. As people in the media heard about us, our story started getting publicized nationally. That really helped us. As we received more and more publicity, we kept growing.

Evan: Initially, our business was strictly mail order. As time went by, and as we received more orders, we expanded it to an actual e-business.

When we were starting out we made a few chocolates at home, but now we make our chocolates at the Denver Enterprise Center. The Denver Enterprise Center provides small businesses with the space and services needed to ensure success. We rent space in the kitchen. It's a commercial kitchen, so we have to meet all the health codes. The Denver Enterprise Center really helped us out by teaching us about health codes [when making chocolate].

Elise: We didn't need much money to start out, just enough to buy the materials for making the chocolate. Because we were on the Web, we didn't have to make a big investment.

We started out buying our materials at craft stores and the supermarket. When we began to need a lot of chocolate and supplies, we started buying wholesale. Now we buy chocolate by the ton.

Evan: With everything that we decide to buy or invest in, price and quality are the main concerns, especially for chocolate. We're in a trial period of looking for the best products to use in our chocolates. Right now we feel that we have a great product that people really enjoy at a good price. It's tasty and cost effective for us.

We don't really have to advertise right now. Occasionally, we do charitable sponsorships, but we are in the situation that we don't have to advertise because we get a lot of publicity from special interest stories. The tagline, "Hey, the Chocolate Farm was started by a couple of kids, and they sell chocolate on the Internet. Go check it out," has gotten us far.

Currently we have twelve part-time employees who make chocolate on a day-to-day basis. We have about another twelve part-time employees who work for us at Denver Broncos games.

K&G: What individual roles do you play in your business?
Elise: Evan is the Internet guy; he handles the marketing and the Web site. I am the chocolate person. I create new products and think of new things to put on the Web site to ship out. It's a company. We each play an important role within the company; without either of us, it would be difficult to manage.

K&G: What is it like to be a kid with a successful business?
Elise: Most people have been really supportive. Sometimes people think our business is not real because we are just kids, but I think being a kid has helped us because it makes us unique.

Evan: When you think of stereotypes, you think of race and stuff like that, but sometimes being a kid can provide its own stereotypes. Our youth has benefited us so much. In some cases, it has given people the perception that we're not real, but everything we do is real. We invite anyone to challenge us to see if our business is real. If you did challenge us, you'd find out that I *do* make the Web site and that Elise *is* a genius when it comes to making the chocolate stuff, and she *does* do all that herself. You know, sometimes you have to challenge the perception and you can't let it get to you. If we ever come across an obstacle, we just keep going. At times other people's perceptions have been a distraction, but they've never been permanent barriers. There are ways of getting around anything.

Elise: We've learned so much. We've learned to follow our dreams, how to run a business, about money, and about chocolate.

Evan: I agree; we've learned how to follow our dreams, take a chance, and be persistent. A lot of the things we did were just the result of seeking knowledge and making mistakes. You can learn a lot if you're willing to make mistakes.

K&G: Who has helped you?

Elise: We've received a lot of encouragement from people we've met along the way, our customers, and from YAB. YAB really supports youth businesses.

Evan: We also received lot of support and help from the incubator where we have our office and the Denver Enterprise Center. We've received information on how to prepare chocolate and how to manage our business after that first step. They really helped us get to the next step.

K&G: What has been the most fun you have had throughout this experience?

Elise: Having this business has been really fun. I enjoy all the people who influence us, like the kids who ask for suggestions about what kind of business they should start. It's been really fun to help them see what their dreams are and have a hand in helping them follow their dreams.

Evan: It's been fun interacting with so many customers, seeing our work out there, getting critiqued and praised, having the power to see how the daily steps we take influence someone, and seeing the power of taking that first step and how big the result can be. Knowing that you have a chocolate business every day is really fun, too. What we like most is that our business is not a job. That's how we think all jobs should be: something that you enjoy so much that you don't really think of it as a job. A job has so many negative connotations of labor and stress and work, and when you're doing something that you enjoy, it's not really a job at all. It's just a fun thing to do, and that's really what we consider the Chocolate Farm to be.

K&G: What has been the least fun you have had throughout this experience?
Evan: The scariest thing about this is going out on our own. Putting ourselves out there is definitely the hardest part—taking that first step. After that first step, a lot of stuff just kind of figures itself out. Having faith in yourself and your dream and following through with an idea can lead to so much success—it's incredible.

K&G: How can other kids start businesses?
Elise: Find something that you love to do. Learn as much as you can about it and then share it with other people. It could become your dream if you really love it. I say, go for your dreams. You'll never know if you don't try. The hardest thing is taking the first step. After that, you'll see what happens. What happens, happens. Just work hard and follow your dreams.

Evan: It's important to let the outside world influence you, but don't let it be the final decider of what you do. You have to be strong and realize that outside views aren't always perfectly accurate. Don't let outside opinion skew your own perception of what you think is right. If you have a dream or a goal and people aren't being as supportive as you'd hoped they'd be, don't let it stop you. That's just an obstacle you have to overcome. You have to stay in touch with yourself. Wayne Gretzky said, "100 percent of the shots that you don't take don't go in." If you don't take that shot, if you don't take that first step, the chances that it will happen are nonexistent. So take that first step, take that risk. Who knows what will happen?

K&G: What is your vision for the future?
Evan: We would like to keep doing this as long as it's feasibly possible. We're having a blast doing it now, and we want to see how big and how great we can make it. We're continuing to grow the company and make it successful and self-funding so that all the basic goals are met.

Elise: We want to continue to create all our products and think up new recipes. We get a lot of suggestions about what kinds of things the customers want. Some people like marsh-mallows or caramels; they send us their ideas and we try them out. We have experimentation time to think of new things, and we have taste tests to see if everyone loves it. If they do, we add it to the product line.

Evan: Our next step is in alignment with our motto, "For those who like to eat and make chocolates." We are expanding our product line to encourage people to make their own chocolate by using our cookbook and newly released chocolate kits. Now we have three diverse products to encourage people to try their own thing. If they want to make their own chocolate, great! We have some free recipes on the Web site and a cool cookbook with some neat graphics that teach you how to make chocolate. We're a little different from traditional companies because we don't hide our secret recipes in a vault. We give all our recipes away for free. We enjoy giving advice and supplying our cus-tomers with the tools necessary to make their own chocolates. It's great if somebody learns something from us; that's fun in itself. Our main goal for the Chocolate Farm is to keep it self-funded. We put all profits back into the business and continue to provide funding for new expansions, new product lines, books, kits, and all the stuff that's associated with running your own business.

It's been my experience that some of the big things that hap-pen to you in life, you don't really expect. Sometimes the stuff you wish for isn't really stuff that you end up getting. Four years ago the Chocolate Farm wasn't even on my mind. The things that have happened since then have been so incredible, you couldn't even imagine. I'm sort of thinking that my next big thing is something that I haven't even thought of yet.

Wrap-Up

If you had asked Elise and Evan five years ago where they would be today, they never would have been able to tell you that they would be running a million-dollar business.

Through their experiences they consistently trusted their inner guidance, they trusted the process, and they trusted themselves and their dreams. Have the courage to trust in yourself, your abilities, and the magic of your dream.

Contact Information
To reach Elise and Evan, go to http://www.TheChocolateFarm.com.

CHAPTER 10

Inner Guidance

Great news! You are not alone on your path. Even when it seems like you are alone, you always have your inner guidance to support and comfort you. Your inner guidance is a built-in mechanism that will help you with your choices along the way—all you have to do is learn how to listen to it!

Let's practice. One way to learn how to listen to your inner guidance is by comparing thoughts or statements that you believe are true to ones that you believe are false. For example, think of your favorite treat. (As an example, we'll use ice cream, but your favorite treat may be something different.) Now think of something that grosses you out. (We'll use liver as an example, but you can choose your own.) While thinking of your favorite treat say, "I love ice cream!" or whatever your favorite treat is. Notice how it makes you feel when you think about eating it. Do you feel excited? Does your mouth water? Pay attention to the feeling in your solar plexus, the area right beneath your ribcage. Notice that you feel comfortable with the true statement you made.

Now think of the food that grosses you out and say, "I love liver!" or whatever yours is. Notice how this false statement makes you feel funny and uncomfortable; you might even feel a knot in your stomach. Practice this a few times with different contrasting examples. As you practice, you'll start to get a feel for the difference between thoughts that are true and feel comfortable to you and thoughts or state-ments that are false and feel uncomfortable to you. This feeling is your body's own inner compass leading you to choices that are best for you.

✍ You can apply your inner guidance to choices you need to make. When you are faced with a decision, weigh your choices by checking your inner compass. Think of each option for your pending decision and say, "_____ is a good choice for me." Notice how it makes you feel. Repeat this exercise with each of your choices. Make a note of which one feels best or most comfortable to you. Try not to think too much about your choices during this exercise. The choice you feel best about is not always the one that seems the most logical. Your head might try to talk you out of following your feelings, but trust your inner guidance. While your head can be clouded by outside influences, your inner guidance is more accurate.

Another way to access your inner guidance is to ask yourself questions and listen to the answer that comes quickly and naturally. Writing is a great method to use for this exercise. ✍ Sit down and write out a question you might have in your chapter. Next, write down the first answer that pops into your head. Don't think about it; just write it. Even if it doesn't make sense, just write it. When you don't stop to think, your inner guidance can speak to you more clearly. If the answer you wrote doesn't satisfy you, write a more specific question. Then, again, write the first answer that comes to you. Repeat this exercise until you feel satisfied with the guidance you have received.

If you would rather take an analytical approach to your questions, simply ask yourself, "Is this choice taking me one step closer to or one step away from my intended goals?" Repeat the question with each of your choices. Listen to the first answer you receive in your head. This is a quick way to find some guidance.

One last approach to listening to your inner guidance is a method that Amanda, our interviewee for this chapter, uses. Amanda says her Angels are her guide. Some believe that we all have angels around us who help us along our path in life.

People who believe in angels say they always guide us without our asking, but you can also ask for specific guidance by speaking directly to them. Simply close your eyes and say, "Angels, I am lost. I need some guidance on _____." Your answer can come to you in the form of a statement that pops into your head or as a feeling, or it may present itself to you through an experience that happens within your day. It may even come to you in the form of a person you don't know who reveals something that might change your perspective and help you find your answer. Be watching and listening. If you need clarity about your answer, just ask for it.

Ultimately you can also ask others for advice. There are many experts in areas where you don't have any experience. Their advice could be quite valuable. Just be sure to weigh the advice you receive and use only the advice that your inner guidance tells you is best for you.

Inner guidance is something that we all use more than we think. It can come as a hunch, a thought, or a feeling. A good way to connect with it is to allow yourself some quiet alone time every day. Learn the art of meditation, a simple process of deep thought in a quiet environment that helps you focus on your own inner guidance and allows you to escape the chaos of all the other voices you might hear. Meditation brings peace to your body and mind and helps you connect to your guidance more clearly. There are many methods of meditation; find one that works for you. If you would like to learn more about meditation, check out our resource chapter for helpful listings.

As you are learning to listen to your inner guidance, be patient with yourself. Don't expect a loud voice to provide you with directions. Inner guidance is often very subtle and may require practice to perceive it clearly. This is where meditation can be very helpful. It helps you get into a more open space where perception will become more clear. The more you use your inner guidance, the easier it will be to interpret it. You may learn to do this right away, or it may take you a while; it doesn't matter—just keep trying. Inner guidance is a tool that will not only help you every step of the way as you work to achieve your dream, but it will help you with choices throughout your lifetime as well.

✍ Do you feel as though you have an idea for how to listen to your inner guidance? Are there times you have used it and it has helped you? Take a minute and write down what happened. Include any feelings or questions you might have about using your inner guidance in your chapter. If you get stuck, read the following interview with painter Amanda Dunbar to learn how she uses her own inner guidance.

LET'S DO IT!

Amanda Dunbar
Age 19
Dallas, Texas

painter

"You can't mess up art. That's what's so amazing about it! There's just no wrong way to do it."

We were lucky enough to interview Amanda in her studio, where we were surrounded by her paintings. Finished work hung on the walls and several unfinished paintings were up in the loft near her easel. Tubes of paint were everywhere. Amanda told us wonderful stories of all her experiences as a painter. We enjoyed hearing about when she was on the *Oprah Winfrey Show*, how she has helped to put art programs back into the local schools, and the personal reactions that people have to her paintings. Amanda not only shared stories with us but she also shared her gift of painting, her views of art in the world, and her ever-present sense of encouragement. Sitting in her personal space, the space where she is oftentimes guided to paint by her Angels, was an uplifting experience. Her paintings show that she is uninhibited, free in her expressions, and free in her emotions, all of which inspired us in our own search for inner confidence and guidance.

Meet Amanda
Amanda had never even thought about painting before she took an art class at the age of thirteen. After that one class, she knew that painting was what she wanted to do for the rest of her life. She became a published painter by the time she was sixteen. A year later her first book, *Guided by Angels*, was published. Now she is known worldwide for her amazing artistry. Her paintings not only sell for thousands of dollars but they also encompass the magic of her message and her gift.

K&G: How did your passion for painting begin?
I started painting in an after-school art class when I was thirteen. I took the class because I thought the teacher was really cool and because a bunch of my friends were in the class. I was not really into sports or music, so I thought maybe painting would be something that I could do. To get us started, the teacher said, "This is the palette, which is the flat surface that you put your paints on to mix them. This is the canvas, a type of fabric that's stretched over a frame, and it is what you paint on," and that's about it. He said, "Play in the paint. Different people start off knowing different things and wanting to do different things on the canvas, so just start painting." I sat down in front of the easel with my palette and my canvas and I just started painting. My teacher had a really interesting reaction to my painting. He had been very enthusiastic and vocal about his support to the other students, but when he came around to look at my painting,

he got very quiet. I thought that I had done something wrong. He said, "Can you do that again?" and I was like, "I guess. I mean, yeah!" I think he thought it was a fluke to begin with, that I just got lucky. I guess it wasn't! I included that first painting in my book, *Guided by Angels*. I knew when I started painting that it was what I was supposed to be doing for the rest of my life. Before that class, I had never had any inclination toward the arts. Since then it's become my life and my passion.

K&G: How did painting in an after-school class turn into a career as a painter?

After the class ended, I just kept painting. Soon people started recognizing my artwork. I started doing gallery shows at the age of sixteen. A gallery show, depending on the size, requires anywhere from forty to fifty pieces of art. Basically, the paintings get put up in the gallery and a lot of people are invited to an opening where you're introduced as an artist and all your work is shown. It's kind of like a big party, and there are a lot of people there. Your artwork is usually up for about a month, but it really depends on the gallery.

At my first show in a Dallas art gallery, I had sixty-eight pieces up. The gallery sold all but two pieces. They could not believe it. They had never had a sell-out show. It was amazing. With the gallery shows came a lot of different media opportunities, including being on *Oprah*. It's just been a whirlwind for me.

K&G: What guides or inspires you to paint?

From the start, I've always felt that there is something working through me, that I'm just an instrument. Soon after I started painting, I realized that my Angels guide me when I paint. I didn't really understand what it was that I was doing, so I haven't always labeled it that way. It feels as if I just know where the colors are supposed to go. It's instinctual. Then people started having emotional responses to my paintings. I can't explain it in any other way.

My family and I have some amazing stories of people coming into the galleries and having incredibly emotional reactions to my work. For example, when I had my very first exhibit, a woman came into the gallery and stood in front of a particular painting for a very, very long time. She said to me, "How did you know? How did you know?" I didn't know what she was talking about. She said, "This is my sister. This is how she looked; this is what she liked to do. This is *her*, and she died three years ago. How did you know this painting was meant for me?" That's just one example of many. At first I thought it was kind of scary and weird. Then it started happening over and over. At each exhibit I've done, I've had a reaction like that from someone. Now I just feel happy that I can *do* that. I think some of my paintings are messages for other people, and I feel very honored to be the instrument of those messages.

K&G: Is there a particular painter who inspires you?

If I had to pick one artist who inspires me, it would probably be either Renoir or van Gogh. When I went to my very first Renoir exhibit, I felt like I knew him, knew what he was thinking, and knew where he was. I knew the places and people that he painted. I think I was fourteen or fifteen at the time. I told my mom, "Wow, look! He paints like I do!" and she said, "No, no, no. I think you paint like *he* [did]!" But I just think I really understand this man. I really understand what he was trying to do. It's a confirmation to me that I'm doing something worthwhile.

With van Gogh, I love his passion—his passion for life, for painting, and for color. I really understand and admire that. I think that he's amazing. I'm very influenced by the Impressionists and the post-Impressionists, specifically Monet, van Gogh, and Renoir, but I'm working on a style that's very distinctly my own.

K&G: How does painting make you feel?

Painting is my happy place. It's where I can think; it's where I can breathe. It's a calming place for me. I love painting. Sometimes it's like a hunger. *It's something I have to do*. Sometimes I get frustrated because I can't get a piece right or I just can't seem to get an idea down just the way I want it, so I work on about six or seven pieces at once. When I get frustrated with a painting, I put it away and start on the next one.

K&G: What type of things do you paint and what mediums do you use to paint?

I like painting things that are representational, which means that you can recognize the things I paint. I think my favorite things to paint would probably be things from my life, things that I see around me that aren't limited to people or landscapes.

Oil on canvas is my favorite medium to work with. I love oil paint because there is a richness to the color and texture that I have never found in any other type of paint. The length of time it takes me to complete a painting depends on its size. It could take anywhere from a couple of hours to a couple of days, to a couple of months.

K&G: What is your vision for your art?

Currently I'm working on two college degrees: one in studio art and the other in art history. My dream is to have an exhibit so big, so different, so thought provoking that it goes down in history. I want my artwork and my movement to be in the history books. I want to change the world with my art, to originate a new way to look at and create art. In a small way, I think I am starting to do that. If I could do anything in the world it would be to spread peace through art. I want to shake the art world; and if it's not me, then I hope it's somebody that I inspire through my foundation, the Angel Alliance.

K&G: What do you accomplish with Amanda's Angel Alliance?

I started a foundation called Amanda's Angel Alliance because I saw a need for art classes. I thought to myself, "You know, if I hadn't had that art class when I was thirteen, what would I be doing right now? My life would be totally different." And the only reason that that art class was available was because my teacher made a commitment to do it.

K&G: How do you feel about the art opportunities available to kids?

I think it's a shame that art classes are the first ones to get cut in school because they're considered frivolous or not important. It's so wrong! Art is something that ties us together as humans. It's something that people have been doing since the beginning of time. I want people to understand how important it is. I believe there's a direct connection between the escalation of school violence and the cutting of art programs. In fact, one child we worked with was a notorious bully. After art became available to him, he did a complete 180. Now, instead of bullying people at recess, he goes into the art room and mixes colors or paints.

K&G: Who has helped you?

My encouragement has come from my parents and my Angels.

K&G: What are your most favorite and least favorite things about painting?

My most favorite thing about painting is that I can convey images to people and they will really look at them. I love that it makes you look at the world in a different way, and it forces you to rethink how you thought about things before you looked at a particular painting. My least favorite thing about art is cleaning the brushes. The scariest time is probably right before an exhibit. Right before you go out into the room, all the people are walking around and you're thinking, "What if they don't like the paintings? What if they're not happy?" That's kind of scary, especially when you're revealing new pieces that are really near and dear to you. It's a little scary to see how they're going to be received, but I've never been disappointed.

K&G: What has been the most fun you have had throughout this experience?

The most fun I've had is walking into a classroom where the people all know who I am and I get to hang out with them and paint with them. I think that's probably one of the best things ever.

K&G: How can other kids become artists?

Start where you feel [inspired]. It sounds kind of silly, but I think you'll just know like I did. So get the paint and don't be afraid to use it and make a mess. You can't ruin art. That's what's so amazing about it. There's no wrong way to do it. Use whatever appeals to you. For me, it's big tubes of paints and a canvas, but if you're more interested in watercolors or brushes or that type of thing, go for it. Whatever really strikes your fancy.

Let the paint inspire you. When kids come to the gallery, I do a demonstration. I do some paintings with them, get out some paper, crayons, markers, paint, whatever, and I draw with them. I think a lot of them are surprised by what they can do themselves and how it makes them feel. Art is a brave means of expression! It's something you can do to get your emotions out or to express yourself. Draw a picture about what the inside of your head looks like right now. What color do you feel like today and why? Draw a picture of your house. Once you get started you'll say, "Wow! You know what? I can do this!"

Don't be afraid of mistakes. When I talk to some of the kids around Dallas, I take two pictures with me. One is a finished painting, ready for display, and the other is an unfinished work. I show the first one and say, "This is what you see in the gallery because this is what I want you to see in the gallery!" I bring the other one out and say, "Not every painting I do is pretty. When you go to the gallery, you see all the finished paintings. I mess up all the time. It's important to realize that you can't ruin a blank canvas. The greatest thing about paint is that you can paint right on top of it."

If you want to paint, just be open. Listen to your heart. Try it; you never know where it's going to lead you. You can be an artist, no matter what anybody says.

Wrap-Up

Amanda has done some wonderful things with her artistic gift. Her Angels are her unique method for receiving the guidance she needs.

Your beliefs will help you find the right guidance match for you. Or you may already have a method of guidance. Have you felt guided by a feeling or a strong sense of knowing that somehow "this is right for me"? Guidance is that invisible force that helps you to know that you are where you belong. Find your inner guidance and feel the magic of believing in yourself.

Contact Information

To reach Amanda, go to http://www.AmandaDunbar.com/.

section 5

Guts

Guts

You have to have guts to follow your dream! Having guts means having the courage to put yourself out there, to let your idea be seen, and to show people your talent. Most of all, it means being willing to make mistakes and move past them. People might say no to you or your idea; they may even laugh at it or tell you that it's not possible. But if they do and you move forward anyway— *that's* guts. If you don't think you have what it takes, don't freak out! You've got more guts than you think—just wait and see!

In this section, to help you to achieve your dream, you will learn the art of using your guts to color outside the lines and find the courage you may not have known you had.

CHAPTER II

Color Outside the Lines

Remember in kindergarten when you were taught to color inside the lines? Well, now that you're older, it's now time to color *outside* the lines. Coloring outside the lines means getting out of your comfort zone, trying new things, and thinking in ways that are unique to you. Remember, lines can be guides or they can be barriers. Sometimes sticking to only one way of doing things can become a barrier instead of a guide.

At times you will probably come up against an obstacle on your way to achieving your dreams. So what should you do if what you are attempting isn't working? Switch directions! Find a different approach or perspective. This is where coloring outside the lines will really help you. It may be easier said than done, but here are several ideas to assist you.

● Be willing to see things differently. You may have an exact plan in your head for how your dream will come to be, but things will almost never turn out exactly the way they look on paper or the way you picture them in your head. Keep an open mind. Don't get set on having something work exactly the way you want it to. Instead of feeling frustrated when things don't work out as you had planned, see it as an opportunity to exercise your creativity, use a new perspective, and make your idea stronger.

● Not getting what you're asking for? Maybe you are and it just doesn't look the way you had expected it to. Sometimes answers and opportunities come to you in different ways than you had imagined. Pay attention to the world around you. Ask yourself how you might be able to look at what is presented to you differently, and be careful not to miss special gifts just because they don't look the way you think they should.

● Ask your inner guide for a new perspective. Take a step back and ask yourself, "How can I look at or approach this situation differently?" and walk away from what you are doing for a while. Sometimes new ideas can come more easily when you aren't so focused on them.

● Look for the bigger picture. It's easy to get lost in the details of a project. When you find yourself getting stuck in the chaos of many details, take a step back and see the big picture. Remind yourself of your initial intention and purpose.

● ✍ When in doubt, brainstorm with someone! Team brainstorming allows you to compile and share ideas with one another. Something happens when you have more than one person working on a project or coming up with creative ideas. Momentum builds and ideas start flying. Use this technique if you need help coming up with ideas. Go to the brainstorming section in your chapter to help you get started.

● Remember to look at all your options, not just the ones that seem easiest or safest. Explore your choices from an objective standpoint. Let your inner guidance help you decide which options would be the best choice for you.

● Study what others have done before you, use their examples as models, then add your own creative spin to it. (Just think about it: people are still creating new and improved airplanes since the first one was invented.)

● Keep going even if you come up against an obstacle. Any dream that is important to you is worth going the extra distance to make it happen.

✍ Coloring outside the lines can be a fun exploration. How do you already color outside the lines in your world?

Do you have any circumstances in your project where you'll need to explore different options? If so, take a minute and write down some ideas for how you could approach these situations with a "coloring outside the lines" perspective. When you are done, take a look at our interview with Laura Lockwood, CEO of ManaTEEN, and discover what it means to have the guts to color outside the lines.

LET'S DO IT!

Laura Lockwood

Age 19
Bradenton, Florida

CEO of ManaTEEN

"I have dyslexia and I was an ADD child, and I wanted to show people that I could do something really great!"

We caught up with Laura in Las Vegas, Nevada, where she was attending a leadership conference with other Mana-TEEN members. Laura appeared to be a little shy at first, but as she talked about her organization she became confident and proud. We enjoyed hearing of Laura's experiences and triumphs throughout her seven years as the leader of the ManaTEEN Club. As she told her story, Laura expressed her need to prove to others that anyone can achieve greatness. Laura has indeed achieved greatness through her abilities to lead, see past obstacles, and change the rules.

Meet Laura

If you met Laura, she would tell you that she has dyslexia and attention deficit disorder (ADD) and grew up being very shy. Some people may say these are not typical characteristics of a strong leader, but they haven't met Laura. She learned to color outside the lines early in life by setting her weaknesses aside and tapping into her strengths and passion. This led her to turn a small volunteer group into the largest teen volunteer organization in the country.

K&G: How did you start your own volunteer organization?
I have to give a lot of the credit to my sister, Kat McKell, for getting the ManaTEEN Club started. She was a senior in high school and I was a twelve-year-old sixth grader. In Manatee County it was mentioned that students might be required to have seventy-five hours of community service in order to graduate from high school. My mom had always run nonprofit organizations, so we were used to doing volunteer work. I knew I didn't want to be in a service club in school; I just wasn't that type of person. I was the type of student who got out of school and came right home. That's when my sister and I decided to go to the volunteer center to ask if we could start a club with our friends.

The volunteer center [representative] said, "You can, but you know, organizations in our community aren't very interested in having teens volunteer unless they hand you a garbage bag or something like that." That information kind of scared us off. With that news, we decided that we just needed to start our own program.

We started by asking a senior citizen who lived next door to us if we could paint her house. She was very excited because she needed her house painted. We were able to get Wal-Mart to donate the paint, and we put up banners to announce what we were doing. Some people wondered if we might be causing trouble, but other people asked if we could paint their houses.

The media came by to see what we were up to. That's actually how we got started. From there we started going to different schools and getting group committees together.

We named ourselves the ManaTEEN Club after Manatee County, where we live. A lot of people actually think that we save manatees, but we don't do that.

At first it was really hard to gain respect from organizations because of our age. It took us a while. Now we work for 486 organizations. In each of the organizations, there's a teenager—a ManaTEEN representative—on the board. It is really great for us. I never would have guessed that ManaTEEN would get this big.

K&G: How does the ManaTEEN Club operate?
ManaTEEN falls under the adult volunteer organization Volunteer Manatee. It has several different programs and we're one of them. It's easier to stay under it than start our own, but we are Volunteer Manatee's largest program.

We are a community-service organization just like any other community-service club, but we're not based in a school. We're based in the whole community, so kids from any school can be ManaTEEN Club members. As of last week we have 11,486 members. We're the largest teen community-service organization in the nation. It's so exciting. It's hard to believe that we started out with just twenty-two members.

We're different than other service clubs. We don't have mandatory hours, mandatory meetings, or fees. You can also be in other service clubs at the same time, and we'll keep track of the hours from those service clubs, too. We keep track of any community service hours you accumulate. We're really like a home base for everybody. I've never even seen some of the ManaTEEN members before because they volunteer alone and report their hours back to us. We receive about twenty-five membership applications each day.

All our teenagers are given leadership roles. If they can think of a project that they want to do, we let them do it. We have officers standing by to help, to encourage them if they fall, or just to give them support. We don't have a lot of adult supervision. People like me are usually around to give the kids as much leadership as possible without bossing them around. We notice that most of the kids really enjoy that freedom.

Our programs include all types of service, from painting houses to cleaning beaches to home safety for seniors, which is currently our biggest program. Rules on Safety for Seniors is really a great program. We work through the Meals on Wheels program, which provides us with contacts to senior citizens who live alone. Rules on Safety started when one of our teens thought of a great idea to help senior citizens who refuse to go to a shelter because they couldn't bring their pet and they live alone. Her idea was to deliver a meal kit with nonperishable food and a flashlight to these seniors. So we started out by going with Meals on Wheels runners to give the seniors this meal kit. We discovered that some of the seniors didn't have lights or had cords all over the floor they could trip on. One of our teens was really concerned about it, so we got money donated to us that we used to buy different safety items to donate to seniors.

After that, Lowe's, which had a grant program for a similar project, heard about us and offered to fund us. Now when we go to a senior's home, the Lowe's Pros teach us what safety hazards to look for. Lowe's donates about $25,000 in safety items that teens deliver to senior citizens. The program has now been replicated around the nation. It's really cool. There are so many projects going on. New programs get created all the time when teens think of them. Our funding comes from grants and donations. We don't do fund-raising, and we never have.

We offer training to all our members. For example, all our officers are trained in opening and managing a shelter in Manatee County. The ManaTEEN Club runs an entire shelter in Manatee County. We offer training in public speaking and babysitting. We give our members credit hours for going to training. Usually the organization that provides the training, like the Red Cross, trains us for free.

We also have Junior ManaTEENS for [kids in] third through fifth grades. It's an after-school program that we're running through two schools right now. Members of ManaTEEN are trained as mentors for the Junior program. They mentor the kids in homework and then they help them do a volunteer project on campus. It could be making emergency meal kits for senior citizens, cleaning the campus, caring for the landscape, or anything they can think of that day. Then the kids have a snack and playtime. The Junior program members can also participate in projects with their ManaTEEN mentors on weekends.

K&G: What role do you play in the ManaTEEN Club?
My role in the ManaTEEN Club now is as an AmeriCorps Promise Fellow. Basically, I work in the office and as a chaperone. We just brought our president and our president-elect on their first trip with us to our conference in Las Vegas.

K&G: What is the biggest change you've seen since organizing the ManaTEEN Club?
One of the biggest impacts in our community has been the increased understanding and respect for teens. I've noticed that ManaTEENS are being invited to traditionally adult luncheons and award ceremonies. There are often awards for ManaTEENs along with the adult awards. I also notice that teenagers are starting to have more self-confidence when talking in front of large groups.

I'm so proud of the fact that we have 11,000 participants in Manatee County. Only about 13 percent of all the teenagers in Manatee County aren't ManaTEENS. Teenagers may not think that Bradenton, Florida, is the coolest place to live, but I've heard so many kids comment on the great organizations there are in Florida that help so many people. They start to respect the town, and, in return, it gives them great self-confidence.

The biggest impact for me personally has been on my shyness. I used to be extremely shy. I still am, but I have a passion for the ManaTEEN club. I really like promoting the idea that youth can do really cool things, especially youth leadership. I've really come out of my shell a lot more than I ever thought I would.

K&G: What was your motivation to start a volunteer club?

I wasn't very popular in middle school or high school. I really wanted a means to get out and meet people. I have dyslexia and was an ADD child, and I wanted to show people that I could do something really great. I also wanted something to motivate me to get through school. That's how I'm going to college now, through scholarships that I've earned because of my community service, not because of my grades. ManaTEEN has been my outlet from school, a place to go and do something good and feel good about myself.

Now my biggest motivation is to tell kids how many scholarships based on your community service are out there. I especially want to get that message out to the kids who are having a hard time in school like I did. I never really made the best grades, and I didn't think that I was going to go to college.

K&G: Who has helped you?

Kat and I started the club together, but then she went to college. Even though she was gone, she was always available for me to talk to. She's been very supportive. I was really scared to do it without her. I thought, "Oh no, I can't do this! I can't keep this going!" My mom was also very supportive of me. I wasn't embarrassed to start a project and then fail miserably because I knew my mom and sister would be there for me and give me advice.

I have to give a lot of credit for our success to the original twenty-two members of ManaTEEN. My sister and her friends had a lot to do with getting us up and going. As a group we just kept thinking of different projects to do, then took baby steps to accomplish our goals. It was really hard, and it didn't just blow up into a huge success overnight. We made sure we told the media what we were doing. That helped us continue to grow and gain recognition.

K&G: What has been the most fun you have had throughout this experience?

Traveling is really cool. I'm able to meet so many people and make friends from different high schools. The most exciting thing to me is to see the bonds that are made through the club. Kids who would never have known each other become friends who go out and do awesome things together. The awards that teens win through their community service are really neat. I get excited to see the officers and the new people who come up with brilliant ideas that I wish I had thought of a long time ago. That's how I know that we're going to last and we're going to stay strong.

The best thing I have done with ManaTEENS was three years ago when I was named a Hasbro Teen with the Courage to Give. Because of that, I met a lot of people from the Hasbro toy company. They have a program where they donate a lot of toys to charity, so I wrote a grant for them to do the same thing through ManaTEENS. Every Christmas, we put an ad in the newspaper to ask if anybody knows of a needy family. We ask for the family's name, address, and the number and ages of the kids. Then our president dresses up like Santa—unless it's a girl president—and we dress up like elves, and go to the family's home and surprise the kids with Christmas gifts. It's so much fun to dress up like an elf and to see the smiles on these kids' faces when we bring a big bag of toys to them from Hasbro.

K&G: What has been your biggest obstacle?

The hardest thing has been getting respect from adult organizations and finding ways to bridge the generation gap so that senior citizens trust us.

K&G: How can other kids start a volunteer organization?

Start at the volunteer center. If your community doesn't have one, try going through your school. You can also start one by yourself.

We always tell people who want to start a ManaTEEN Club in their community to contact us on our Web site, and we will give them our handbook, all our program ideas, and all the support we can. When other volunteer centers want to start a teen club, we sometimes travel to that location to help them replicate our club. We can't tell people what to do, but we can definitely tell them what not to do because we've been through it.

K&G: What is your vision for the future?
My initial vision for this group was just to have a group of friends, meet new people, and do community service. That was really all I thought it could be. Then one day we found out that we were the largest community-service group for teens in the nation. I want to show people that youths can do really cool things.

I see ManaTEENS staying strong, and I'm really excited to see other groups grow as much as we have. I know that each community is different, so everything will work out differently for each one, but I hope ManaTEEN keeps its status. I never want to leave my baby, but I know I'll have to. I'm working with the ManaTEEN Club right now through AmeriCorps while I go to school. I don't know what will happen after that.

As a ManaTEEN founder, my biggest dream is to see the club blossom, to keep Manatee County as beautiful as it is, and to keep the awesome bonds we've created with the adults and senior citizens.

Personally, my biggest dream is to be an archaeologist and to work for a museum. I'm going to school right now to achieve that dream. My dad is an archaeologist, so I've grown up with that. I also want to go into nonprofit management.

K&G: Do you have a message for other kids?
My message, especially to kids who have learning disabilities and who struggle a lot or have a hard time believing in themselves, is that you can still do really great things. I've

seen a lot of things change for me because of the service club, things that I thought would never happen for me. I thought that school was the only way to be successful. I really feel that the training and the experiences I've had in the club have given me a better perspective on the way things work. I'm not so scared anymore to go out into the real world. I think I'm the most self-conscious person in the world, and to have this huge club to run, to support and promote it, has been really hard for me. But it's forcing me out of my shell, and I'm stomping the whole way.

Wrap-Up

Examples and guidance were offerd throughout this chapter on how to color outside the lines—how to use new ideas and per-spectives to create something wonderful. Laura came across people who were unable to change their perceptions of what a teen volunteer could be or accomplish.

Laura chose to not let her ability to do well be limited by someone else's opinions. Have you come across similar situa-tions? Create your own possibilities by accepting nothing less than "I can do anything!" When an obstacle appears in your path, don't allow it to limit what you want to do. Switch direc-tions, make new rules, or just decide that you will not settle for less than the dream you really want to attain. Color your own picture.

Contact Information

To reach Laura, go to http://www.ManaTEENs.org/.

CHAPTER 12

Courage

It's time to be gutsy—to take action! Without action your dream can never be realized. Taking action to follow your dream requires courage—having the willingness to be the authentic you, trying new things, believing in yourself, and never giving up. This book can give you a strong foundation of courage from which to launch any idea or dream. Remember, the only person who has enough power to come between you and your dream is you!

If you ever find yourself needing extra courage for a difficult task, you can program your mind to release the fear so that you can complete the task with ease. Make it a goal to overcome your fear and expect success. Try using repeated visualizations of the smaller steps required to accomplish your task. This is a little different than the other visualizations you have worked with because here you will break the main task down into smaller tasks. This process is important because it conditions your mind to feel comfortable with each step within the task.

Imagine you need to make a presentation at school and you're nervous and unsure of yourself. Conquer your fear by dividing this task into smaller steps and visualizing them in positive ways. With each step, repeat the visualization until your nervousness subsides.

- **Step 1:** The first small step can be walking out the door to go to school on the day of your speech. Visualize yourself walking confidently, looking forward to doing well. By repeatedly imagining this moment, you will become more comfortable with it.

● **Step 2:** Visualize the moment when you walk through the front door of your school. See yourself feeling happy about the presentation you're about to give.

● **Step 3:** See yourself walking into the auditorium where you will perform your speech. Imagine that you look great, you feel confident, and you see smiling faces around you.

● **Step 4:** See yourself starting your speech confidently. You feel relaxed, the words are coming easily, and you know you are doing well.

● **Step 5:** See yourself gaining momentum in your speech, having a great connection with your audience, and finishing with a feeling of success.

● **Step 6:** Visualize yourself about an hour after your speech. It feels great to be finished and to know you've done a good job. Focus on this feeling of victory.

Now, in your head, you've already walked yourself through each step and have successfully completed the speech. So when it comes to the actual event, you can connect with the feeling of accomplishment that you have already felt and imagined many times. ✍ Use the visualizing techniques with any task that you need some added courage for. Space is provided in your chapter to give this exercise a try.

As you go along in your life, you will find that having courage is a natural part of who you are. You may not always feel brave. You may even feel like you fear a lot of things, such as change, new surroundings, new experiences, differences, or even yourself. Fear of the unknown is very common, but you don't have to allow it to keep you from going after what you want. Remember that you are the one in control of what you believe; you are in control of your courage.

Determine success by measuring what is in your heart. Keep your eye on your game and only compare your results with your previous results. You may feel happy because you conquered a fear, or because you were able to get the information you needed, or because you accomplished one of your goals. The point is, you are successful in that moment. Celebrate the courage in it.

If you need more guidance with courage, allow the teens in this book to be your inspiration. Each was chosen because of the courage he or she demonstrates. They all have their own way of saying, "I believe in me, and I will not let anyone or anything stop me from living my dreams."

As you were guided through this book, you may not have realized that you were guided to find your courage, but each element of TeenVision is a component of it. To have a dream and believe in that dream and yourself, to create something from your inner gifts that you can share with others, to discover your inner strength and to investigate, to invest in yourself and to find confidence, to be inspired and to inspire others, to trust in yourself and your inner guidance, and to color outside the lines—that is courage.

Create your core foundation of courage by believing in yourself, then build up from there. Build upon each moment's success. Feel good about this moment and then see yourself successful in the next. Add each of the attributes as you are ready for them. Before you know it, you will have developed something that has always been a part of you—the courage to do anything you dream of!

Read our final interview with Justin Lewis and Matthew Balick to see how the importance of having the courage to follow through with an idea can lead to a lot of fun.

LET'S DO IT!

Justin Lewis and Matthew Balick
Ages 13 and 14
Chicago, Illinois

Inventors of Flip-Itz

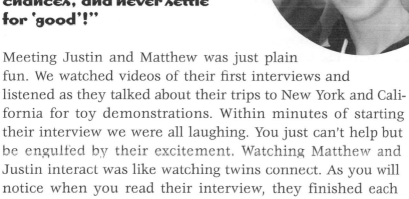

"If you have an idea, don't just keep it in the dust. Try to expand it, take chances, and never settle for 'good'!"

Meeting Justin and Matthew was just plain fun. We watched videos of their first interviews and listened as they talked about their trips to New York and California for toy demonstrations. Within minutes of starting their interview we were all laughing. You just can't help but be engulfed by their excitement. Watching Matthew and Justin interact was like watching twins connect. As you will notice when you read their interview, they finished each other's sentences.

As we interviewed Matthew and Justin, we both realized how important it really is to keep fun in any project. Even though fun is an important element in your dreams, sometimes it takes courage to have fun amidst new experiences.

Meet Justin and Matthew
Justin and Matthew have been friends since kindergarten, which is for more than half of their lives. They both have such a high level of energy that they light up a room when

125

they are together. Their friendship exudes fun. In fact, they came up with a great idea for a toy while just goofing around. Coming up with a great idea is one thing, but following it through and making it into a real toy is extraordinary. Their company, called Two Bored Boyz, was born and a great new toy, called Flip-Itz, was launched.

K&G: How did you come up with Flip-Itz?
Justin: We invented Flip-Itz when we were eight years old.

Matthew: We were at a banquet for our basketball league. The person running it was taking a long time, and we were waiting for everyone to get settled.

Justin: We were hungry!

Matthew: Yeah, we were hungry. After [waiting an hour] they gave us pizza and we ate, [but] we were still very bored. So we took out the three-legged stand that keeps the box from squishing the pizza, and we started playing around with it. We started flipping it and before we knew it . . .

Justin: . . . before we knew it, everyone at our table was starting to flip them—kids our age, my parents, and Matt's parents were all flipping them. Matt and I thought they would make great toys! We asked our parents to help us with this idea and they agreed. From there, we started our company and called it "Two Bored Boyz."

Matthew: For the actual Flip-Itz, we started off with the original three-legged stands that we had saved from the pizza boxes. Then we started thinking about how we could take it a step further to make it an actual toy, rather than just a stand.

K&G: What was involved in creating a company from your original idea? Did you have help?
Justin: It took maybe two years to get our company up and going with the new product.

Matthew: Sales were very slow at the beginning, but once it got started it became a little . . .

Justin: . . . a little popular. Flip-Itz basically sold out of stores, and it was very hard for us to manage the company on our own.

Matthew: Especially because we were in school and our dads were at work all day. Because of this, we signed a contract with a small toy company to help us market and distribute our toy.

Justin: Next we created different types of characters and games to expand the toy. We created a Flip-Itz packet and then went to toy demonstrations and expos to demonstrate how the toys work. Publicity increased after we got interviewed on a radio show in Chicago.

Matthew: It wasn't a very big radio station, but I remember that was one of our first publicity opportunities.

Justin: As far as characters go, a few months ago there were twenty-four [Flip-Itz] characters, but now we have about forty and there are more coming.

K&G: How are the toys designed and manufactured?

Matthew: We design the characters and games first, then have them manufactured. To come up with new characters and games, our whole family helps. First we have brainstorming meetings where even our sisters think of characters. We have also come up with ideas just from playing around with the Flip-Itz. In the beginning, we would think of stuff to play, like Flip-Itz golf. The first one to the end in the least amount of strokes wins.

Justin: There was a game called Flip-Itz 21 [where you try to earn exactly twenty-one points]. [The score] depends on how the Flip-Itz lands; that's basically the point of the game.

Matthew: The characters are made from molds. So we'll think of . . .

Justin: . . . we'll think of what characters we would like, and then we bring them to our manufacturing company to see what they can do with it.

Matthew: We'll think, let's make an elephant and call it Stomp. Or we'll just have an elephant and then we'll think of ideas for how to make it different, and then sometimes artists will take care of how it looks. But also we . . .

Justin: . . . we give our ideas for it. My favorite character is Huey the Horse because he flips high and he's really funny. My favorite game is either Basketball, where you try to get the character into a hoop, or Flip-Itz 21. Actually, I like all the games. I can't really choose.

Matthew: Yeah, I can't choose with the games. I like Huey the Horse and I like the Leapster, which is a frog, and Limber Louie.

K&G: Who has helped you?

Justin: Our families have supported and encouraged us a lot with Flip-Itz.

Matthew: Mostly our dads. They put things aside just to take us to demos and to help us think of new ideas. They've always been there for us.

K&G: What has been the most fun you have had during this experience?

Justin: Going on trips has been the most fun. We've been to Texas, California, and New York. New York was the most fun because it was our first trip and we were on a lot of television shows. California was also fun because we were on the Disney Channel and went on all the rides at Disneyland.

Matthew: Yeah, we had a lot of fun going to New York and Los Angeles. We were in New York for more than week. We walked around, bargained with street vendors, and had fun goofing off. In California we were at Disney to film a movie they were making to take around to schools. We got to work with the guys who do Radio Disney and Mark and Zippy.

Justin: Everything has been a great experience.

Matthew: We go to toy demonstrations to show companies how Flip-Itz works. The demos have been kind of hard sometimes because it can take a long time to travel to them. They can be two hours away.

Justin: But it's worth it. They're really cool. I like them.

K&G: What do your friends think about Flip-Itz?
Justin: Our friends think it's great. They don't . . .

Matthew: . . . they don't think of us in a different way. Some-times we'll go to stores and our friends will kind of embarrass us by telling the store people that we invented Flip-Itz, trying to get them to give us free toys. But the store people never believe us.

K&G: How can other kids start a toy company or invent a toy?
Justin: Start with the basics. Think of ideas, characters, and themes or what the toy could do.

Matthew: Your invention doesn't have to be a toy. Once you have thought about what you want to invent, find a grown-up you can trust to help you. Kids don't have all the connections that adults do, so find an adult to help and start from there.

Justin: If you have an idea, don't just keep it in the dust and say, "I don't think it will work." Actually try to do it. Try to expand it and improve it. Then maybe it will become a success.

Matthew: Take chances and never settle for "good." Try to keep making it better and better until you succeed.

K&G: What is your vision for Flip-Itz and your company?

Justin: Our dream is to expand Flip-Itz and see what happens from there. It would be awesome to get it into new stores.

Matthew: And bigger stores. We really want to get it into a big pizza company.

Justin: A small pizza company uses them now, but we want to get our product into a bigger pizza chain.

Matthew: Domino's would be a great place. The whole point is to offer Flip-Itz as collectable characters. It could even help attract kids as business for the pizza company. The kids would want to collect Flip-Itz, and buying the pizzas would give them that chance.

Justin: We would like Flip-Itz to excel and become a better toy.

Matthew: I agree with that. I also think the experience that we have had is good enough. Obviously, the majority of kids out there don't get this opportunity, to go through all this and get a sense of the business world.

Justin: It feels really awesome, because if we see Flip-Itz in stores, we think, "Wow, that's our toy," and we're really proud of it.

Matthew: Since we dissolved our partnership with the toy company, our next goal is to find some new people to help us market and distribute Flip-Itz. It is an awesome toy. We know it can be a big success.

Wrap-Up

Justin and Matthew are two boys who love to have fun. They had the courage to believe that an idea inspired by boredom could be a real toy sold in stores. They were inventive and creative. Getting their idea into production involved more work than they had anticipated, but they found their own individual courage to help them follow through with their idea.

The next time you are in a boring situation, let your imagination go and see what new ideas you can come up with. Imagine the possibilities and remember to have courage (and fun), throughout the process.

Contact Information

Justin Lewis and Matthew Balick
Two Bored Boyz
P.O. Box 1117
Deerfield, Illinois 60015

section 6

vision

My TeenViʌion

This is your chapter! It's all about you. When you fill it out, remember that there is no right or wrong way to do it!

As you go through your chapter and your life, make sure you include fun as a major element. Having fun while expressing yourself, your passions, your vision, and your dreams will make for a fun and exciting life. So get your pencil ready, put on a smile, and begin creating the life you want to live!

On the first page, there is room for you to place your picture. If you would rather make a collage by pasting affirmations or magazine pictures and words, that's great, too. Decorate it! Have fun and be as creative as you want to be!

Here are some quotes and affirmations to get you started. Cut them out or write them onto your pages.

"The most powerful thing you can do to change the world is to change your own beliefs ... and begin to act accordingly."
—Shakti Gawain

"You must be the change you wish to see in the world."
—Mohandas Gandhi

Dream

Successful, I am

"It's kind of fun to do the impossible."
—Walt Disney

I can do ANYTHING!

"Go confidently in the direction of your dreams. Live the life you've imagined."
—Henry David Thoreau

"Keep away from people who try to belittle your ambitions. Small people always do that, but the really great make you feel that you, too, can become great."
—Mark Twain

"Take the first step in faith. You don't have to see the whole staircase, just take the first step."
—Dr. Martin Luther King, Jr.

I believe in my dream

"Whether you think you can or think you can't—you are right."
—Henry Ford

Strong, I am

Go for it!

"You must do the thing you think you cannot do."
—Eleanor Roosevelt

Confident, I am

Place your picture here or make a collage:

CHAPTER 1

What are your visions and dreams?
Highlight or mark with a star the dreams you feel most excited about.

What is the dream you are most excited about?

cHαρterз

Make a list of terms that describe yourself.

My strengths are:

My weaknesses are:

My unique qualities are:

Things I'm good at include:

Words that best describe me are:

Negative thoughts/beliefs thoughts I have about myself:	**Positive replacement I have about myself:**
Example: I can't play sports.	Examples: I am willing to try anything, including sports.
	I can learn anything.
	I love a challenge.
	I am willing to take a risk and have fun, no matter what.

Make a list of the beliefs you have about your dream. Be honest with yourself. If you have negative beliefs, be aware of them so that you can find replacement beliefs. Include any fears or doubts about this process as well.

CHAPTER 3

Write down everything you imagine your dream to be. Imagine how a day living your dream would be. Include what that day would look and feel like.

What are some of your unique talents or natural abilities?

What are some of your unique personality traits? Think of the most obvious ones that people might see in you when they first meet you. Some examples of these might be compassion, a great sense of humor, a passion to help others, strong confidence, or great communication skills.

Write down the inner gifts and talents your dream is built around.

What is your purpose with your idea or project?

What is the motivation behind your dream/idea?

Now that you have your dream well defined, what supplies or items will you need to make it happen?

CHAPTER 4

Answer these questions for yourself. Be sure to answer honestly.

Do you have the courage to be an original, to do things your own way?   Yes/No

Do you know that you can accomplish any life goals you might have?   Yes/No

Do you stand up for yourself when necessary?   Yes/No

Do you refuse to allow other people's opinions affect your success?   Yes/No

Do you keep striving for new goals?   Yes/No

Do you know that you can depend on yourself when times get tough?   Yes/No

What are some examples of ways you have used your inner strength?

Imagine meeting someone who doesn't like your idea and tells you that you should just throw in the towel. How can you use your inner strength to overcome this obstacle?

For each item on your supplies and items list from chapter 3, create a list of places where you could get your items or who you can ask for advice or help. These will be your resources. As you create your resource list, you may find it helpful to keep a file folder for the papers that you may collect, such as business cards, catalogues, phone numbers, pictures of products that you want to reinvent or improve upon, or just a list of additional resource questions. If you are doing research on the Internet, create a special folder in your bookmarked favorites labeled "resources." This will help you find them again.

**Supplies /
Items needed**   **Resources / Name**   **What / Who**

Web address   **Phone number**

Who is someone you would like to research who might inspire you? Research people or companies that have had experience doing something similar to what you want to do. Use their paths as models for ways to accomplish your own dream.

CHAPTER 6

Write down your short- and long-term goals.

My Short-Term Goals	Date Set	Anticipated Date of Completion

My Long-Term Goals	Date Set	Anticipated Date of Completion

Make your goal setting FUN! Make a goal collage. Find pictures and phrases that represent your goals and tape or paste them onto this page or create your collage on a new piece of paper.

List as many steps and actions that you can think of that will help get you started on your dream or idea.

Steps I need to take

Example:
Find a supplier for caramel

Find member for
volunteer group

Actions I need to take

– Go to grocery store
– Research wholesalers on the Internet and
in the phone book
– Order samples to taste quality

– Ask friends and have
them ask more friends to join
– Create and distribute flyers
– Ask school principal if we can announce
that I have started a volunteer group and
need members

CHAPTER 7

What does your body language tell people around you?

How are you communicating your ideas?

What is your excitement level?

Are you being true and honest?

Are you being yourself or who others want you to be?

Are you proud of your ideas or embarrassed and shy about them?

How do you handle making mistakes or bad choices?

Write a goal you would like to visualize yourself accomplishing.

Affirmations help! Talk to yourself when you first wake up, talk to yourself in the shower, tape affirmations to your mirror or write them in your journal. Create a positive space in your mind that will keep you pumped up no matter what anyone else says to you. The idea is to tell yourself what you need to hear.

Examples:

Confident, I am.

Successful, I am.

Proud, I am, of myself and my choices.

Special, I am.

Strong, I am.

Amazing, I am.

Beautiful, I am.

An amazing gift, I am.

Examples: Positive Self-Talk:

I love my creativity.

I love my uniqueness.

I can achieve anything
I dream possible.

I love how well I communicate.

I love how quickly I can
solve problems.

I love my talents.

Anything is possible.

I love my sense of humor.

I love being a risk taker.

I believe in me.

When someone important to you makes a suggestion to "improve" an idea that you have, what would you do?

What would you say to the person?

What are some ways you can feel more confident?

CHAPTER 8

What can you say or do to convey your passion for
your idea to others?

Fun ways I can stay connected to my inspirations are:

CHAPTER 9

How has trust played a role in your life or in your current project?

Trust plays a role in my life in this way:

I know I can trust myself to:

I know I can trust myself in future situations because:

I know I can trust myself with my current project because:

Ways I would like to learn to trust myself more are:

CHAPTER 10

What decision are you faced with?

Decision to be made:

List your possible choices:

Now state each choice in this way:
_____ is a good choice for me.

Choose the option that feels best or most comfortable to you.

Write down your question. Directly below it, write the first answer that pops into your head. Don't think about it; just write it down. If your answer doesn't give you the guidance you need, ask yourself another question. Thens write down the first answer you think of. Repeat this until you feel you have the guidance you need.

Examples:
I need guidance in finding my inspiration.
I need guidance in selecting quality people to help me with my project.

How can inner guidance further your dream? How have you listened to your inner guidance in the past? What was it like? What happened?

CHAPTER 11

Need an infusion of new ideas for your dream or project? Brainstorm with at least one other person using these ground rules:

● No idea or comment is bad or wrong.

● When you get an idea, share it.

● There are no other rules!

Start by letting everyone know where you need some extra help. Let them know what ideas you have already tried, if any, and where you are stuck. Give everyone a piece of paper to write down some ideas. Everyone has ten minutes to write down anything that comes to mind, even if it seems silly. (That silly idea could be what changes everything.)

Gather everyone's notes and read through all the ideas. Talk about the new ideas. Talking about ideas creates synergy and brings creativity into the group. Throw around other ideas. Remember, no idea is bad. Be creative! Use your imaginations. Step outside the box and outside your comfort zone.

New ideas I could explore for my project include:

How do you already color outside the lines in your world? Are there any alternative roads you could take while working toward your dream?

CHAPTER 12

Try this exercise to help you turn fear into excitement!

The event or task that has me a little scared is . . .

Now break it down into smaller steps. (Use as many steps as you need.)

The day of my event or task, I imagine myself starting the day by . . .

The next step I visualize myself doing is . . .

The next step I visualize myself doing is . . .

The next step I visualize myself doing is . . .

Finally, I visualize myself completing . . .

Now that you have your visualization steps written down, create a routine for yourself. In the days or weeks before your task, use these visualizations to settle any anxiety you may have. Try seeing and feeling yourself change from being anxious to being excited about the experience. You can and will do anything that you believe you can.

Repeat this process for anything that you are afraid of. As you work through your fears you will realize that you feel empowered. This feeling of empowerment can help you to overcome obstacles and allow you to get even closer to achieving your dreams!

Resources

Here's a little extra guidance through what may be new territory. Know that your path is as unique as you are. When you read these books by and about other people, take away what feels right to you. You are your own leader. Take chances when finding your passion. Know that you only need to believe in you and your ability to achieve. Live your life with joy and happiness and be sure to have a lot of fun along the way. What follows is a list of books, Web sites, and Tips & Tricks to help you on your way toward success.

Dreams – Chapter 1
BOOKS
The Young Entrepreneur's Edge: Using Your Ambition, Independence, and Youth to Launch a Successful Business (Princeton Review Series) by Jennifer Kushel
This book includes key topics such as "tricks of the trade," obtaining capital, and writing a business plan, as well as how to get older people to take you seriously. Although this book is geared toward the eighteen-to-twenty crowd, it contains invaluable strategies specifically for the young entrepreneur.

What Should I Do with My Life? by Po Bronson
The author traveled the world to find people who have searched for and found their true calling. This book is about finding yourself amidst the routine of daily life and realizing that your calling has been coming to you as a whisper, rather than as a complete package labeled "your

destiny." Bronson wrote, "We all have passions if we choose to see them." Although this book is primarily for adults, it can be enjoyed by teens as well.

The 7 Habits of Highly Effective Teens by Sean Covey
This book is fun! Covey knows that sometimes reading can be boring, especially if you have to learn something from it, so he placed cartoons, quotes, clever ideas, and inspirational stories about other teens throughout his book. Read and have fun while you learn to be an effective teen!

The Totally Awesome Business Book for Kids by Adriane G. Berg and Arthur Berg Bochner
Through fun quizzes, games, cartoons, and stories, this book helps ten- to seventeen-year-olds start a business. You'll enjoy all that this book has to offer.

WEB SITES
The ManaTEEN Club http://www.manateens.org/
This volunteer club was founded by teens. Check out its Web site and get ideas to use for your own nonprofit club. If you don't find all the answers to your questions, e-mail manateens@aol.com.

Kids Care Clubs http://www.kidscare.org/
This Web site will help you learn how to start a club in your local community by holding charitable events.

TIPS & TRICKS
Find what makes you excited or inspired and explore opportunities that include this excitement. Who knows? Maybe you will create something new that no one else has created yet!

Believe – Chapter 2
BOOKS
What Do You Stand For? A Kid's Guide to Building Character
by Barbara A. Lewis
This is a huge book with lots of examples of kids and what they stand for. If you need some help in figuring out who you are and what you believe in, this is the book for you. For those of you on the debate team, this book has tons of great topics for discussions.

Self-Talk: Key to Personal Growth by David A. Stoop
If you don't talk positively to yourself all the time, *Self-Talk* may be the book for you. Learn how to tackle negative self-talk with this delightful book.

The Magic of Thinking Big by David J. Schwartz
Even though this book is directed toward adults, it is a valuable teen read. Schwartz shows that thinking big can bring big results. He also teaches the reader to learn and understand the habit of thinking and behaving in ways that will get you where you want to be. Look for the sections that appeal to you and don't get overwhelmed by the thought of having to read every word. Read what you are attracted to and don't worry about the rest.

TIPS & TRICKS
Broaden your belief system by taking time to discover the beliefs of others around you. Ask questions that are based on issues that are important to you. For example, if spending time with your dad every Sunday is important to you, your question for someone could be, "Do you have any rituals of spending time with your family?" As you ask others about their beliefs, remember that you are on a learning expedition and are not there to judge their answers. Learn from others and open yourself up to the different beliefs around you.

Create – Chapter 3
BOOKS
Gifted Girls: Activities Guide for 365 Days of the Year: Fun Things to Do for Kids and Grown-Ups That'll Develop Creativity, Social Skills and Self-Confidence! by Kailin Gow
This great book will help spark your creative side and keep you from running out of ideas.

WEB SITES
Kids Philosophy Slam   http://www.philosophyslam.org/
The Kids Philosophy Slam was created to help kids find their philosophical voice. This contest makes philosophy accessible and fun for kids of all ages and abilities. Pre-registration is required. Make sure you check out this site for the deadline and topic for the current year.

By Kids For Kids (BKFK)   http://www.bkfk.com/
Explore this site and find tons of help and information related to inventing. An annual invention contest is available to club members.

Talented Kids   http://www.TalentedKids.com
This is a great resource for kids to find information on subjects such as acting, modeling, and animals. It also showcases kids' talents. On this Web site, kids can connect with other kids their own age who might live in their area or even around the world.

TIPS & TRICKS
Each day, try to create something—it doesn't really matter what. Try different things and think big. Instead of writing in a journal, write a story. Instead of painting on a piece of paper, paint a mural on a wall. Instead of singing in your room, put on a concert for your friends or relatives. There is no right or wrong way to create—just create! It's all up to you.

Inner Strength – Chapter 4
BOOKS

Boys Who Rocked the World: From King Tut to Tiger Woods by Lar DeSouza

Girls Who Rocked the World: Heroines from Sacagawea to Sheryl Swoopes by Amelie Welden
If you were asked, "How will you rock the world?" what would your answer be? Find your inner strength and share your gift with the world, just as the people highlighted in these books did.

Stick Up for Yourself: Every Kid's Guide to Personal Power & Positive Self-Esteem by Gershen Kaufman Ph.D., Lev Raphael Ph.D., and Pamela Espeland
Need a little help with your self-esteem? Through the exercises presented in this book, you will learn about your own feelings, dreams, and needs. You will also learn to stick up for yourself, become responsible, and make good choices.

TIPS & TRICKS
Look into taking a class in martial arts to help you find your inner strengths. The philosophy behind martial arts is to instill discipline and self-confidence. Try yoga for a softer approach.

Investigate – Chapter 5
BOOKS
The Business Start-Up Kit: Everything You Need to Know about Starting and Growing Your Own Business by Steven D. Strauss
Here is everything you need to know about starting your own business. It's geared toward adults but beneficial to all.

Business Kit for Kids: A Complete Start-Your-Own-Business Kit for Kids by Summit Financial Products and Michael J. Searls

This book is for kids ages ten to sixteen and is a great resource to learn about the basic principles of money and finance.

The Young Entrepreneur's Guide to Starting and Running a Business by Steve Mariotti

This book is one of the best guides for starting and running a business. It not only has stories about adults in business, but it also has stories of kids in business. And it includes many examples of different types of businesses and available resources.

WEB SITES

Internet Public Library http://www.ipl.org/

This is a great place if you can't get to your own local public library. There is a special place just for teens called TeenSpace.

The United States Chamber of Commerce

http://www.uschamber.com

Are you searching for a local business and just don't know where to look? Try calling your local chamber of commerce. It's a powerful resource for community information.

TIPS & TRICKS

Practice asking questions. Join the school paper or conduct surveys as if you were a reporter. Come up with different questions to ask people and then arrange the questions and answers into a story or an article. The more questions you ask, the better equipped you will be in knowing which questions will get you the information you need.

Invest in Yourself – Chapter 6

BOOKS

Meditation for Kids (and Other Beings)
by Laurie Fisher Huck

This book is great for the person who has never meditated before. The author explains that meditation is a way of discovering who we are and a way to stop, listen, and quiet the mind from the restless energy of life.

Teach Yourself to Meditate in Ten Simple Lessons: Discover Relaxation and Clarity of Mind in Just Minutes a Day
by Eric Harrison
Learn the core practices of breathing, body awareness, visualization, and much more. If you really want to develop lifelong meditation skills, this is the book for you.

What Do You Really Want? How to Set a Goal and Go for It! A Guide for Teens by Beverly K. Bachel
Make goal setting fun. Learn to set priorities, overcome obstacles, and build a support system. This book is a step-by-step guide to goal setting. Each chapter includes fun, creative exercises, practical tips, words of wisdom, real-life examples, and success stories.

TIPS & TRICKS

When you invest in yourself, you invest in your future. Take time to give yourself what you need. Take some quiet time, me time, playtime. Be sure to give your ideas, dreams, or projects the time and energy they need as well. Take a meditation class. Take up a new hobby to get your creative juices flowing. Life is meant to be FUN! Create a life that is surrounded by the things you love.

Confidence – Chapter 7
BOOKS/CARDS

Power Thoughts For Teens by Louise L. Hay
These fifty brightly colored affirmation cards are a great way to build your confidence. Pull out a few cards every day. Take them with you and read them throughout the day or hang them on your mirror.

What to Say When You Talk to Your Self
by Shad Helmstetter, Ph.D.
Create the energy to turn your dreams into reality by knowing what to say when you talk to yourself. This book takes the concept of affirmations and creates powerful self-talk that will empower you to achieve your goals.

The Confidence Course: Seven Steps to Self-Fulfillment
by Walter Anderson
Positively transform your life through the Confidence Course. Anderson teaches you how to determine what you want to be and where you want to go. This is an invaluable read for anyone searching for his or her passion.

How to Develop Self-Confidence and a Positive Self-Image Permanently and Forever (audiocassette and workbook)
by Michael S. Broder, Ph.D.
With Broder's book, you will develop self-confidence and a positive self-image in no time.

WEB SITES
Teen Ink http://www.teenink.com/
Get published as a teen writer! Teen Ink is a national teen magazine, book series, and Web site devoted to teen writing. Teen Ink helps teens share their stories about their lives. Keep an eye out for the monthly contests.

TIPS & TRICKS
Confidence comes from within, and there are many things you can do to build it. Doing things for others is one way to make yourself feel good. Help your mom or sister, or maybe your teacher or another student at your school. Another way to build confidence is by doing what you are good at and what makes you feel proud.

Inspire – Chapter 8
BOOKS
Chocolate for a Teen's Dreams: Heartwarming Stories About Making Your Wishes Come True by Kay Allenbaugh
This book focuses on the importance of following your heart. These real stories show how desire and determination can turn a vision into reality, and the writers offer advice for when things don't turn out according to plan.

Better Than a Lemonade Stand: Small Business Ideas for Kids
by Daryl Bernstein
This book, written by a fifteen-year-old, gives you ideas on how to create a small business for yourself.

How to be a Teenage Millionaire by Art Beroff and T. R. Adams
If you want to be an entrepreneur, then why not shoot to be a millionaire? This book has many great stories of adults and seventeen teen entrepreneurs and their achievements. You will have no problem finding someone to model after, and the book includes tons of resources for you to explore.

WEB SITES
Amazing Kids! http://www.amazing-kids.org/
This Web site is dedicated to helping kids through education and projects. It features Amazing Kids of the Month every month and even allows you to nominate yourself or a friend. Check out the mentor and scholarship programs as well.

MENTOR: National Mentoring Partnership
http://www.mentoring.org/
This Web site helps in every aspect of mentoring. It will hook you up with a mentor, help you become a mentor, or help you create a mentor program in your area.

TIPS & TRICKS
Inspiration can be found in the oddest places. A painter may see a person's face and instantly want to paint it, and an inventor may see many possibilities in a simple piece of plastic. Look everywhere for your inspiration. If you are a writer, observe people in a park. If you are a dancer, watch how gracefully birds fly. Find inspiration everywhere in your daily life.

Trust – Chapter 9

BOOKS

Trust in Yourself: Thoughts About Listening to Your Heart and Becoming the Person You Want to Be by Donna Fargo

Do you believe that you can move mountains if you believe in yourself? This book inspires you to trust yourself and to inspire that trust in others. Using your heart and soul as a guide, learn to listen to what they are telling you.

WEB SITES

Young Americans Center for Financial Education and Young Americans Bank (YAB) http://www.yacenter.org/

YAB helps kids become knowledgeable about managing their financial affairs and so much more. This bank was created specifically for people twenty-two years old and younger. YAB is in Colorado but has customers all over the United States (via checking by mail). Advantages to banking with YAB include a lower deposit requirement (minimum of $10), customer service geared toward kids, and money management and investment programs for local kids. The support given to teach kids how to manage their money is unbeatable. Check out the Web site to become a customer or for help on how to manage your money.

TIPS & TRICKS

Trust can appear tricky. Ultimately, the act of trust is based on first trusting yourself. By putting yourself in leadership roles, you will learn how to trust your ability to make choices and decisions. Run for class president or form a group with your friends and assign each responsibilities that must be followed through. Exercises like this will help you both make decisions and learn to trust your choices.

Inner Guidance – Chapter 10
BOOKS
Writing Down the Days: 365 Creative Journaling
Ideas for Young People (Revised and Updated)
by Lorraine M. Dahlstrom, M.A.
Need a little help with journal writing? This book gives you a whole year's worth of creative writing assignments. Don't worry, these are nothing like school assignments. Questions such as "What's your favorite thing to do when you have the opportunity to do 'nothing'?" are fun and meant to get you thinking about the possibilities in life.

Intuition for Starters: How to Know and Trust Your Inner
Guidance by J. Donald Walters
This book gives you exercises and guidelines that will help you tap into your intuitive guidance.

TIPS & TRICKS
The best way to hear your inner guidance is to learn how to be silent. Give yourself time each day to turn off the TV, the radio, and the computer. If you can, go to the mountains, the beach, or a nearby park. Away from distractions, you can then just listen and observe. Open your mind to the different thoughts that flow through, but try not to judge anything around you. You can close your eyes to make this step easier. Learn to just appreciate the moment. Allowing yourself to be silent each day is a gift to yourself that will allow you to connect with your inner guidance.

Color Outside the Lines – Chapter 11
BOOKS/CARDS
Who Moved My Cheese? for Teens: An A-Mazing Way to
Change and Win! by Spencer Johnson, M.D.
This book opens your eyes and challenges you to consider if you've been doing only what is easy and indulging in your comfort zone, rather than living your life to its fullest. This is a fast and easy read, and you'll have a lot of fun with the book's characters, Hem and Haw.

Thinkpak: A Brainstorming Card Deck
by Michael Michalko
Need a little extra help with your brainstorming sessions? This is a great and fun way to brainstorm. These cards will help you get out of your head and tapped into your creative energy.

TIPS & TRICKS
Stretch your imagination and come up with a new way of doing something. Look around you. What can you improve upon or change? Jot down your ideas. Everyone has his or her own way of doing or creating things, but how would you do it? How would you create it? Just as clothing designers have to revamp clothes each year, add your own flare to a project and come up with something new. Experiment with different things. Create a new Rollerblade or design a stuffed animal that no one has seen before. The whole point is to color outside the confines of someone else's ideas.

Courage – Chapter 12
BOOKS
Feel the Fear and Do It Anyway by Susan Jeffers, Ph.D.
Have you ever asked yourself, "Can I handle this?" This book asks and teaches you how to have the core belief of "I can handle anything."

The Wonderful Wizard of Oz by L. Frank Baum
This is a great story about finding yourself and having the courage to be proud of who you are.

VIDEO/DVD
Willie Wonka and the Chocolate Factory
by Warner Home Video
You may think that this story is just for kids, but think again; it really makes you feel that you can do anything! This is a fantastic story about a boy who has enough courage to trust his own belief system. He's not swayed by his circumstances and doesn't let others influence or change his values, and he emerges the winner in the end.

TIPS & TRICKS

Learn to take risks. These risks can be small or they can be big. Each time you take a risk, you will learn more about yourself and find courage that you never knew you had.

Take a risk and try something you have never done before. The type of risk that we are talking about isn't the dangerous kind; it is the kind that gets you to do something new. Maybe you could join a club, talk to a new group of kids at school, learn a new language, or try out for the school play. Opening yourself up to trying new things helps you discover more of your talents and inner gifts, and allows you to gain courage each step of the way toward living your dream.

More Fun Resources to Check Out

BOOKS

The Book of Lists for Teens by Sandra and Harry Choron
Gather some friends and read this book together or read it by yourself. It's fun and thought provoking. With more than 250 lists, you are sure to find several items that relate to you and your life.

Awaken Your Birdbrain: Using Creativity to Get What You Want by Bill Costello
Don't passively wait for inspiration to pop into your head. Read this book for creative techniques and gain the tools you need to be creative. Costello believes that creativity is a key element to achieving happiness and success. He has also written a kids' counterpart to this book, titled *Creativity for Kids of All Ages.*

WEB SITES

Camp Resource: Online Summer Camp Directory
http://www.campresource.com/
Find a summer camp that fuels your passions. Choose from a variety of camps focused on art, adventure, sports, travel, and so much more.

TIPS & TRICKS
Enter Contests

There are contests in writing, drawing, inventing, photography, and lots, lots more. Whatever your special interest is, chances are there is a contest for it.

When entering contests, make sure you check out the contest rules written in the fine print. It may not be that much fun to read the rules, but it could make the difference between being a winner or not. If you are under thirteen, there are special rules that companies have to abide by. Go to http://www.ftc.gov/ for more information about the Children's Online Privacy Protection Act (COPPA) of 1998. And have fun! There are many creative contests out there for you to try your hand at, like art, painting, photography, and writing. You name it, there's a contest for it—and for you.

Thanks to all the dreamers out there who are everyday inspirations for the rest of us.

Thanks to all the kids in this book and around the world who are willing to take risks to follow an idea or a dream and share their brilliance with us.

Thanks to all the parents of the kids of *The Road to TeenVision* for allowing us into your homes and your hearts.

Thanks to all the readers of this book who open themselves up to all the amazing possibilities that exist within them and in their world.

Kristi: Thank you, Mom and Norm, who have put up with me for so long and have gone above and beyond in offering support and guidance. Thank you to all my friends and family who have come along on this journey and supported me along the way.

Gidget: Mom, you have such a giving and caring heart. Thank you for your unwavering support and your belief that I really can do anything. Jean, you have a special place in my heart. Thank you for your support, love, and kindness. Norm, Sr., you are a special man, and I thank you for helping me through the lean times! My brother, Joe, thank you for your help. Although you thought I was crazy for quitting my great-paying corporate job, you helped me anyway. And thank you for picking us up when the RV broke down in Tucson. To my brother-in-law, Bruce, I thank you for your help on the original Web site and for hosting PlanetGiggle.com. To Aunt Janice, thank you for supporting my risk-taking adventures! And to each one of my friends who sent money, spread the word about the Web site, or let us park the RV in their driveways, thank you!

National Cover Contest

Nadia Virani

Age 13

Friendswood, TX

Congratulations to Nadia, our national cover contest winner! Nadia's cover is a reflection of what TeenVision means to her and we are proud to feature the unique design in our book. We look forward to seeing Nadia's future artistic accomplishments.

Please see our Web site for more contests: www.planetgiggle.com

Kristi and Gidget

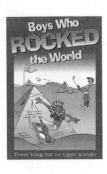

HEY BOYS! WHY WAIT FOR SUCCESS?

Did you know:
- Galileo invented the first accurate mechanical clock at the age of eighteen?
- Bill Gates founded his first computer company and invented a machine to solve traffic problems at the age of sixteen?

Boys Who Rocked the World not only shares the stories of boys who have made a difference in the world before the age of twenty but also profiles boys currently preparing to take the world by storm. Are you one of them? The world is waiting to be rocked by you!

160 pages, black and white art, $8.95 softcover

HEY GIRLS!
SPEAK OUT • BE HEARD • BE CREATIVE • GO FOR YOUR DREAMS!

Discover how you can:
- Handle grouchy, just plain ornery adults
- Avoid life's most embarrassing moments

✳ Scholastic & Book of the Month Club Selection ✳

Girls Know Best celebrates girls' unique voices and wisdom. Thirty-eight girls, ages seven to fifteen, share their advice and activities. Everything you need to know from the people who've been there: girls just like you!

160 pages, black and white collage art, $8.95 softcover

ARE YOU A HERO?

This empowering collection of biographies will inspire kids and adults everywhere to see the world in a new way—as a place where one person really can make a difference.

142 pages, black and white art, $9.95 softcover

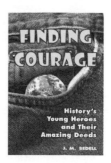

HEY ADVENTURERS!

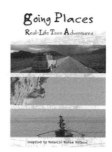

What's the farthest place you've ever traveled? Going Places takes you on exciting trips where kids just like you overcome fears, take on new challenges, and eat weird foods . . .

- Join Pamela Edgeworth as she tries to survive a week of boot camp.
- Venture with Hannah Jackson to an eco-farm in Ecuador.

Going Places will make you curious about traveling outside of your comfort zone.

152 pages, black and white art, $9.95 softcover

To order or to request a catalog, contact
Beyond Words Publishing, Inc.
20827 N.W. Cornell Road, Suite 500
Hillsboro, OR 97124-9808
503-531-8700

You can also visit our Web site at *www.beyondword.com*
or e-mail us at *info@beyondword.com*.

BEYOND WORDS PUBLISHING, INC.

OUR CORPORATE MISSION
Inspire to Integrity

OUR DECLARED VALUES
We give to all of life as life has given us.
We honor all relationships.
Trust and stewardship are integral to fulfilling dreams.
Collaboration is essential to create miracles.
Creativity and aesthetics nourish the soul.
Unlimited thinking is fundamental.
Living your passion is vital.
Joy and humor open our hearts to growth.
It is important to remind ourselves of love.